The Emerging New Order in Natural Gas

The Emerging New Order in Natural Gas

Markets versus Regulation

Arthur S. De Vany and
W. David Walls

QUORUM BOOKS
Westport, Connecticut • London

Library of Congress Cataloging-in-Publication Data

De Vany, Arthur S.
　　The emerging new order in natural gas : markets versus regulation
　/ Arthur S. De Vany, W. David Walls.
　　　p.　cm.
　　Includes bibliographical references and index.
　　ISBN 0–89930–944–5 (alk. paper)
　　　1. Gas industry—United States.　2. Natural gas—United States—
　Marketing.　I. Walls, W. David.　II. Title.
　HD9581.U5D43　1995
　　338.2'72s85'0973—dc20　　　　94–46198

British Library Cataloguing in Publication Data is available.

Library of Congress Catalog Card Number: 94–46198
ISBN: 0–89930–944–5

First published in 1995

Quorum Books, 88 Post Road West, Westport, CT 06881
An imprint of Greenwood Publishing Group, Inc.

Printed in the United States of America

The paper used in this book complies with the
Permanent Paper Standard issued by the National
Information Standards Organization (Z39.48–1984).

10 9 8 7 6 5 4 3 2 1

Copyright Acknowledgments

The authors and publisher gratefully acknowledge permission to reprint the following:

Figure 3.1: From De Vany, A. S. and Walls, W. D. (1994c) Open access and the emergence
of a competitive natural gas market. *Contemporary Economic Policy* 12(2):77–96. Permission granted courtesy of Western Economic Association International.

Figure 4.2: From De Vany, A. S. and Walls, W. D. (1994b) Network connectivity and price
convergence: Gas pipeline deregulation. *Research in Transportation Economics* 3:1–36.
Permission granted courtesy of the original publisher, JAI Press Inc.

Table 6.3: From Walls, W. D. (1994c) Price convergency across natural gas production
fields and city markets. *The Energy Journal* 16(1). Permission granted courtesy of the
International Associations for Energy Economics.

Contents

II   The Evolution of Markets   **39**

Tables and Figures

TABLES

FIGURES

Preface

Economists usually write their books in the hope that other economists and their graduate students will find them useful. We share that hope. We have aimed this book not only at economists, but at a wider audience of readers who are interested in how institutions shape the performance and structure of industries.

This book is about how the natural gas industry transformed itself when its regulators finally authorized competition and markets. The remarkable transformation of this industry can teach us how markets and competition emerge and coevolve, and also what institutions have to be built along the way.

Our story is about the growth of spot markets and the coming to maturity of the natural gas pipeline grid. It is about how the regionally scattered spot markets opened when pipelines switched to transporting gas. It is also about how these regional markets became more strongly connected in a growing network of markets, how they became less segmented, and how their prices converged.

The transformation of the natural gas industry was brought on by regulatory crises that forced deregulation in various stages, first of wellhead pricing, then of gas contracts, and, eventually, of pipelines. As markets responded to the opportunities presented by these changes, they forced still more regulatory adaptations until the industry reached a stage where gas buyers and sellers could deal directly with one another, for the first time in history, and arrange with a pipeline to carry the gas they traded. These innocuous changes brought competition and markets to an industry where they had been repressed for more than fifty years.

Competition and markets rule the natural gas industry now and the market is pricing and allocating natural gas with a graceful adaptability and precision that no regulator could ever hope to approach.

The changes that are under way in natural gas are precursors for deregulation and market-driven systems in other industries. One of our aims is to learn from the evolution of the natural gas spot and futures markets what may lie ahead for electricity and other industries that share characteristics with natural gas.

The newly organized structure of the gas industry is built on access to the pipeline transmission network and decentralized markets, and this structure can be adapted efficiently to many other industries that have network characteristics: electricity, oil pipelines, airports and airlines, bank networks, trucking, shipping, railroad terminal markets, commodity exchanges, and telecommunications industries. By studying how the natural gas industry evolved markets at all levels of the network and how the trading of network access supported this evolution, one could learn something of how these industries could evolve more flexible and adaptive ways of operating.

We hope that energy and natural resource researchers and practitioners will find the book to be of interest by virtue of its subject matter and because of our method of analyzing the way institutions affect how the industry operates. Regulatory economists should find our discussion of the emergence of industry structure of interest and we hope they will find beneficial our somewhat novel view of natural monopoly in a network of markets. Our theoretical models and statistical evidence form a rather new way of looking at arbitrage in markets with network structure.

This book grew out of our collaboration over a three-year period, beginning with David Walls's dissertation, for which De Vany served as principal advisor, and continuing in a series of individually and jointly authored papers published in various journals and books. Some of that work is summarized here, though much of the material is new and the synthesis of the arguments and evidence is entirely original to this work. The book was written in the summer of 1994 in Irvine, California, and in Hong Kong. In a real sense, it was written on the Internet, which seems a fitting way to do a book on networks.

Arthur S. De Vany

W. David Walls

Acknowledgments

For Bonnie and Amy, our natural energy sources.

Our thanks to our employers, the University of California, Irvine and the University of Hong Kong, for providing inspiring places to work. We wish to acknowledge the University of California Transportation Center for assistance to Walls and the Institute for Mathematical Behavioral Sciences, University of California, Irvine and the Private Enterprise Research Center of Texas A & M University for assistance to De Vany. Thanks to Robert Michaels and Rodney Smith, who introduced De Vany to the natural gas industry in a pleasant and stimulating earlier collaboration. We alone are responsible for the book's contents.

Part I

The Emergence of Markets

Chapter 1

The Transformation of Natural Gas

The natural gas industry in the United States is undergoing a transformation from the planned and centrally controlled industry it had become after more than fifty years of federal and state regulation to an industry whose organization and function is based on markets. The old regulatory institutions are failing and new market institutions are under construction. Natural gas suppliers, pipelines, and customers are all part of the process that is transforming the industry. It is passing from an era of planning and regulation by central control and command to one in which market forces and freedom of choice reign.

The transformation of the natural gas industry is a natural experiment that we can use to gain a deeper understanding of how regulation and markets work. The remarkable transformation of this industry can teach us how markets and competition emerge and coevolve and what institutions have to be built along the way. We can follow this transition and use it to test the theories and arguments that have been advanced over the advantages and disadvantages of regulation versus competition in an industry long characterized as unsuitable for competition.[1]

The story we tell is about the emergence and evolution of the natural spot market as it began in the production fields, spread to the pipeline interconnection points and city gates, and came to maturity with the opening of the futures market. We discover how the evolution of the natural gas market was linked to the structure of the natural gas pipeline grid, which became more interconnected and open as pipelines became transporters rather than sellers of natural gas.

The transformation of the natural gas industry was brought on by regulatory crises that forced deregulation in various stages, first of wellhead pricing, then of gas contracts, and, eventually, of pipelines. As markets responded to the opportunities presented by these changes, they forced still more regulatory adaptations until the industry reached a stage where gas buyers and sellers could bypass the pipeline to deal directly with one another and arrange for the pipeline to carry the gas they traded. The power of choice, expanded by an increasing number of paths between buyers and sellers which an open network of pipelines provided, brought competition to every open point in the network.

The gas market has evolved a network structure. The network of markets draws on the pooled resources of production fields throughout North America by linking them all to the pipeline network. The wide participation of buyers and sellers in many markets that are interlinked throughout the pipeline network gives the market a high degree of liquidity and graceful adaptability to shocks. The market is pricing and allocating natural gas today with a precision that no regulator could ever hope to approach.

The newly organized structure of the gas industry is built on access to the pipeline transmission network and decentralized markets, and this structure can be adapted efficiently to many other industries that have network characteristics. Electricity, oil pipelines, airports and airlines, bank networks, trucking, shipping, railroad terminal markets, commodity exchanges, and telecommunications industries all share the network characteristics of natural gas markets. By studying how the natural gas industry evolved markets at all levels of the network and how the trading of network access supported this evolution, one can learn something of how these industries could evolve more flexible and adaptive ways of operating.

At a deeper level, the experiment we follow here in natural gas is a test of the idea that decentralized markets work better than centralized planning. We rediscover in natural gas what many in the United States thought we already knew, and which the collapse of planned economies in Europe gave evidence of; namely, markets work better than planning. This book is about how the invisible hand replaced the visible hand of regulation in the natural gas industry.

THE NATURAL GAS INDUSTRY

There are three sectors in the natural gas industry: production, transmission, and distribution. The production of natural gas is focused in a few areas, primarily in the Southwest of the United States. From wells in these producing fields, gas is collected and transmitted through pipelines to users. From the pipeline, the gas is transferred to a system of pipelines through which it is distributed to users. There are many ways of organizing production, transmission, and distribution, but only one of these has dominated the industry. This organization is principally the creation of regulation and the boundaries of regulatory authority.

In terms of organization, production, transmission, and distribution are separated, with each function performed by a separate business organization or firm. There is little vertical integration between these sectors within the industry. Production and transmission have been divorced for some time, so that pipelines do not produce gas. Nor do producers own pipelines, beyond local connections to the trunk line. Distributors, too, are separate from pipelines, and they do not produce gas.[2] Gas distributors typically take gas out of the interstate pipelines at state boundaries; they are wholly state operations and, therefore, are subject to state and local regulatory commissions.

Pipelines own their facilities "down the line" from the collection system to the point of transfer to a distributor. They are not horizontally integrated over components of the pipeline grid; that is, no pipeline owns enough links in the grid to connect regions beyond the narrow corridor which their line traverses. Pipelines do not own route networks like airlines; they own narrow corridors from a few supply points to a number of distributor customers downstream. Before the changes that were made by the Federal Energy Regulatory Commission's (FERC) open access rulings, the pipeline was a link in a supply chain from a field whose resources were dedicated by contract to that line to the distribution company which was obligated by contract to buy gas from the pipeline. All that is changed now.

A BRIEF HISTORY OF REGULATION

Of the three possible forms of transmission service that pipelines could have offered—merchant carriage, contract carriage, or common carriage—regulation mandated that they be structured as integrated merchant carriers that sold gas bundled with transportation.[3]

Regulation suppressed markets by organizing the natural gas industry along the lines suggested by the theory of natural monopoly: a single pipeline was authorized to link a city market with a producing area; entry was limited; transportation tariffs and gas prices were controlled; customers were unable to deal directly with producers because pipelines were required to be merchant carriers that owned the gas they transported; gas sales were arranged through long-term contracts. Because of these restrictions, gas markets failed to exist.

Merchant Carriage

During the 1930s the natural gas industry was vertically integrated to a significant degree. In some cases producers owned pipelines. In other cases, distributors owned pipelines and production facilities in the gas fields. Under the Natural Gas Act, Congress reorganized the industry as a system of separate merchant carrier pipelines, divorced from production and distribution.

Vertical integration was discouraged, entry was controlled, and pipeline tariffs and gas prices were regulated.[4] Pipelines were required to tie the sale of gas to its transportation and could not offer pure transportation to their customers. Pipeline customers, usually local distribution companies and large end users, could purchase only the bundled package of services that included gas acquisition, storage, and transmission. Two qualities of bundled service were offered, interruptible deliveries and firm (uninterruptible) deliveries.

Certification

The process through which federal regulators certificated pipeline construction led to a dense, but disconnected, network of pipelines. Individual pipelines were constructed as new supplies were found and as the demand for natural gas increased. The Federal Power Commission (FPC) certificated construction of a new pipeline only after it had shown that it had reserves to supply its downstream customers for a period of fifteen to twenty years. To achieve this end, pipelines entered long-term contracts with producers under which the reserves in the gas wells were dedicated to the pipeline. Pipelines could not be abandoned, and contracts could not be renegotiated without the approval of the FPC.

This certification process balkanized gas markets. It created a disconnected network topology which prevented gas from flowing from each connected field to each connected city. The cities and producing fields connected by pipelines were isolated from the fields and cities connected by other pipelines. Pipelines operated independently of one another, each supplying the cities to which it connected with its dedicated gas supplies.[5] The disconnected network topology and limitations on trading prevented markets from existing and blocked competitive arbitrage between points of supply and use.

Open Access

Despite regulation that attempted to maintain high levels of reliability to users, federal price controls caused shortages of natural gas in the 1960s and 1970s.[6] In response to these shortages, Congress passed the Natural Gas Policy Act in 1978. The act deregulated the field price of gas in steps and completely deregulated the price of some types of gas. In 1979, there was a major interruption of world oil supplies. Reeling from gas curtailments, a run-up in oil prices, and uncertainty over the deregulation of field prices, many pipelines signed long-term contracts to buy large volumes of gas at high prices. When gas prices fell after well-head prices were deregulated, these pipelines faced infeasible minimum purchase obligations of high-priced gas. Many of them renegotiated their contracts with producers. In exchange for partial release from their purchase obligations, these pipelines offered to transport gas for producers, or their customers—this was the beginning of open access transportation in gas markets.

The FERC approved these transportation transactions individually until October 1985, when it issued Order 436 permitting interstate pipelines to transport gas for others under "blanket certificates." This regulatory order formally distinguished and separated the pipeline merchant and transportation functions.[7] After some initial skepticism, pipelines began to make application to become "open access" pipelines. The number of pipeline applications and approvals for open access carrier status grew rapidly from 1985 to 1990. Three years after the issuance of Order 436, nearly all the major pipelines were open access pipelines.[8]

Unravelling Regulation

Maybe we owe something to the Organization of Petroleum Exporting Countries, because when oil prices ran up and came down in the 1970s and then again in the 1980s, the structure the regulator and its experts designed broke apart under the stress. Nothing they did was right. They forced the industry to act and structure its dealings as though the nation were running out of natural gas. They predicted shortages and high prices and made the industry prepare for the worst. When the break came and energy prices tumbled, pipelines, suppliers, and customers were caught in a web of contracts that could not be sustained. The total value of commitments in the industry exceeded the value of its resources at the new prices of energy. They tried to find ways of adapting to the onslaught of these changes. The market gained a toehold and the rest is history.

Some say the regulators helped to lead the way, but they were, at first, trying to save their skins for they had created a situation that was intolerable for everyone and they had Congress demanding a fix. But, each new fix stressed the archaic structure in a new place and the stresses spread so quickly that regulators were chasing a moving target. After well-head prices were deregulated, there was a brief run up in gas prices and then a lasting decline set in that brought natural gas spot prices down to levels that were far below the prices consumers were paying for regulated gas. The truly embarrassing part of this was that there was no way to lower prices to consumers under the contractual obligations that pipelines had taken on and which the regulators had approved and were obligated to uphold. The pipelines had taken on large contracts for gas during the period just before the price fall at the insistence of regulators and forecasters; these contracts then stood in the way, so pipelines became the villains in the play.

Breaking Contracts

The contracts that obligated distribution companies to buy the gas they had agreed to take were abrogated by the FERC as Congress angrily threatened to change how pipelines could do business. Pipelines were merchant carriers who bought and sold gas, taking ownership of each shipment that went through their lines. Congress threatened to turn them into common carriers. Instead, pipelines were given the option of becoming contract carriers. If they did this, they would be permitted to sell gas they could not otherwise sell and some of their heavy contractual obligations would be relieved.

In order to make this plan work, another set of gas contracts had to be eliminated. The deal the regulators offered was that they would abrogate part of the pipeline's contracts to purchase gas with producers, if the pipeline would agree to operate as a transporter of gas. In this way, gas and transportation were unbundled—one could buy either one separately. The pipeline would transport gas purchased by any customer who had a contract to buy gas from it. The customer could buy the gas from anyone for the best price and the pipeline would carry it under contract. In return, the pipeline was relieved of part of its contractual obligation to purchase gas at the old high prices.

The End of Regulation?

Events reversed the roles of regulation and markets in natural gas; the market now seems to be driving regulation and it is forcing it to be more honest and adaptable. The paradox is that even while the market is taking over the burden of gas pricing and allocation formerly handled by the Federal Energy Regulatory Commission, the staff and budget of the commission are expanding at an unprecedented rate. Is this evidence that the FERC is driven by the market and needs a bigger staff to remain current? Or does it need the bigger staff to patch the unravelling fabric of regulation and to hold together the coalitions that support it? Based on what we have learned about natural gas, we like to think the FERC is in the death throes of a feedback loop in which its ever-expanding budget and ever-diminishing usefulness are driven by markets to a point where it can no longer sustain the interests that support it.

Choices and the Network

Customers had choices and suppliers were in competition for their business. They could arrange their best deals without having the pipeline or the regulator in the way. Then they could bring the deal to the pipeline which would transport the gas. So many pipelines were open that there were many paths through the network for buyers and sellers to come together. This is where our research comes into the story.

TRACKING THE EXPERIMENT

A big part of the story is how the industry reorganized itself, given the degrees of freedom permitted to it. No one designed how gas was to flow through the pipeline network, and the organization of the network under contract transportation was fundamentally created by the participants themselves. They created market centers as places to trade and new market institutions to govern how they traded and to coordinate their gas trades with transportation.

The success of this transformation hinged precisely on relaxing just a few aspects of how transactions for gas and transportation were structured. The emergence of contract transmission, direct dealing between buyers and sellers, and the evolution of a highly connected pipeline network are the fundamental forces that drive the ongoing natural gas industry transformation.

Links in the network give structure to interrelations between markets. Where links are absent or not open, the spot markets in that segment of the network will operate differently from the others. We can measure directly the connectivity of the network, and we can relate it to the spatial distribution of prices in the spot markets scattered on it. Because arbitrage requires open paths between markets, the spatial distribution of prices will be a superposition of the connections in the grid. Where a path between markets is not open, those markets will not be as closely connected to the other markets in the network and prices will reflect this. By looking at the spatial distribution of prices and its dynamic, we can infer where the grid is connected and where there are isolated components within the grid. So, our general theoretical approach is to model adaptive pricing in a connected network so that we can learn from the spatial distribution of spot prices and its dynamic behavior how well the gas market is working.

The book is in three parts. Part I sets the stage; it describes the industry and how it was organized and frames the debate over markets and regulation. It describes the transition to markets and the emergence of competitive markets and institutions in place of regulatory institutions.

SUMMARY OF PART I

Regulation in Theory and Practice

In Chapter 2, we briefly cover the history of the industry and how it was regulated. We summarize the principal elements of the theory of regulation and distill propositions that we can test in tracking the performance of markets. We show how the ideals of efficiency and equity on which the normative theory of regulation is based were implemented in practice. In grappling with the overwhelming complexity of the task, regulation simplified and segmented the problem by dividing the industry into separate, smaller and more comprehensible pieces that balkanized the industry and institutionalized monopoly. These segmented structures freeze adaptation and block efficient function.

Emergence

Chapter 3 sets the stage for the industry transformation that began in the late 1970s. In it we discuss the history of regulation in order to understand how it shaped the industry's structure and operation and brought it to the crises that led to its transformation from a centrally directed industry to one that is organized through decentralized markets. We also critically discuss the theory of regulation in light of what we know about how the industry worked before it was regulated and how it works now that it is partly deregulated.

SUMMARY OF PART II

In Part II, we follow the evolution of the spot and futures markets.

Fields and Hubs

In Chapter 5, we trace the evolution of spot markets in the production areas. Our concern is with understanding how the spatial distribution and dynamics of prices evolved as these markets progressively were embedded in a larger web of open pipelines and interconnected markets. One important factor in this evolution was the emergence of "market centers" for gas and transportation trading at the places where pipelines intersect or pass so close to one another that a short link is all that is needed to connect them. These centers connect the network and make possible the flexible routing of gas that allows shippers to contest many markets from any supply point. Another crucial factor was the attainment of a connection structure that opened enough paths in the network to arbitrage to force a transition of the segmented spatial markets to an integrated natural gas market.

Our empirical examination of natural gas spot prices in twenty spatially separated markets leads us to conclude that gas markets became more strongly integrated from 1986-1987 to 1991. The spread of open access through the grid was not uniform and the pattern of market cointegration shows discontinuities that match the opening of key pipelines. By 1991, more than 65 percent of the markets had become cointegrated. The increased cointegration of prices is evidence that open access has made gas markets more competitive.

City Gates

In Chapter 6, we follow the gas as it moves beyond the production area and pipeline pooling centers to the city gates. We ask how closely prices at the city gates are linked with prices in the production fields and pipeline hubs. Are the local delivery systems and the gate between the local distribution system and the interstate network sufficiently open so that spot prices at city gates are subject to the same kind of arbitrage forces that we found at work between the production areas and pipeline hubs?

We show that a few city gates are well integrated with the production area markets; however, most are not as well integrated as they could be if the city gates were completely open access. Open access pipeline transportation and partial bypass at the city gate have brought prices at most, but not all, city gates into line with prices in the fields. Prices do not stay within the narrow limits that one finds between the fields and market centers. It is not distance alone that makes the difference, for very distant market centers are highly integrated with production fields and their prices track one another closely. It is access through the city gate that matters and the gate is not open far enough yet. City gates also lack the sorts of market institutions that serve the interstate market so well.

City gate markets need have little fear that their prices will be too strongly influenced by local conditions, perhaps with the exception of the capacity-constrained Southern California city gate. Local volatility is quickly damped by the network and its links to the pool of gas throughout its points of supply.

Futures Market

Because spot prices are volatile, a futures market can promote greater efficiency by allowing gas users and suppliers to hedge against the risk of future price changes. A futures contract permits sellers and buyers to lock in future prices, even though their deals are made in a volatile spot market. If they can hedge price risk effectively through futures contracts, they will be less reluctant to rely on the spot market. Moreover, an organized futures market is a mechanism for discovering price where trades are documented and the delivery mechanism is well known. For all these reasons, a futures market can promote a better spot market. Has the futures market done this? That is the question we address in Chapter 7.

The pipeline network is sufficiently open to assure the deliverability required for a futures market. We find that the futures contract supplies an effective hedging mechanism in many markets, though there are many other markets for which this determination remains to be made. There are some regional markets that show price behavior that makes the futures contract a less satisfactory device for hedging there than at other locations.

The good news is that the futures market is alive and well and its price discovery mechanism is reliable and unbiased. The futures market price is an unbiased predictor of the future spot price at its point of delivery. And it is an unbiased predictor, up to transmission cost differences, of spot prices at most other markets. The contract offers gas suppliers, users, and traders an effective hedge against price risk and a good estimate of where gas prices are headed.

SUMMARY OF PART III

In Part III, we try to draw the lessons for policy that the experiment teaches.

Lessons

In Chapter 8, we look back on the theory of regulation versus markets from the perspective gained from our study of the emergence and performance of markets in fields, hubs, city gates, and futures. The propositions that we drew from the debate between regulation and markets are informally tested here in an attempt to assess the theory of regulation. Most of the propositions fail to stand up. There are two compelling failures in the theory of regulation: it fails to predict how the industry really works under regulation, and it is absolutely incorrect in its predictions about how competition works.

Markets succeeded because open access gave them scope to operate, let new kinds of traders join the market, and gave traders the means for directly trading with one another over wide areas. Open access enlisted the power of networks to discipline markets.

Open access was instrumental in eliminating entry barriers. Transportation trading make it possible to enter and exit a market quickly and without making irreversible commitments. A supplier who wishes to contest a market need not construct a new pipeline to do it and so they no longer are faced with the high fixed costs of entering and exiting markets. Thus, the "hit and run" entry of contestable markets theory (Baumol et al., 1988) has been put in place in gas markets by allowing gas and interruptible transportation to be actively traded among a variety of participants.

Open access, along with the development of effective market institutions, was highly effective in connecting the transmission network and supporting the competitive trading that promoted the convergence of formerly closed and segmented regional markets to one market.

Policy

In Chapter 9, we close the book by asking how the experiment can guide policy. We look at how policy can promote the evolution of firms and industry organization so as to reshape the pipeline network to adapt to new circumstances and increase the efficiency of gas markets. The emphasis is on how firms and the industry can be restructured to use network resources. We argue that an improved transportation right would complete the transition to a competitive gas industry. An effective and adaptive natural gas industry demands new and flexible institutions. It is unlikely that these institutions can be designed by regulators or other "outside" policy makers. We must turn access to networks into an asset.

Design by policy makers founders on the complexity of the design problem. Policy that aims at a social optimum is too vague. Policy that aims at a specific goal is too narrow. The attempt to optimize policy for a given goal produces a narrow optimum that lacks robustness and may be far from optimal when circumstances change. Our conclusions? Remove natural gas from the political agenda and turn it over to market forces.

Successful innovations in industry institutions and organizations are more likely to come from the interactions of the participants in the process; in other words, efficient institutions are more likely to be self-organized rather than handed down from above.

NOTES

1. For example, F.M. Scherer in his classic industrial organization text cites pipelines as "reasonably clear examples" of natural monopoly (1980, p. 482).

2. There are exceptions to all these points, but they accurately characterize the dominant structure of the industry.

3. See Daggett (1955) for a discussion of the various forms of carriage.

4. Mulherin (1986a, 1986b) shows that the Federal Power Commission created a disincentive for pipelines to integrate vertically into the production fields and instead use long-term contracts. However, De Canio and Frech (1993) provide empirical evidence that these contractual arrangements were consistent with economic efficiency.

5. Both the Civil Aeronautics Board and the Interstate Commerce Commission chose similarly fragmented structures for the industries they regulated.

6. See MacAvoy and Pindyck (1975) for a study of the economic effects of federal price controls.

7. Earlier orders had already dismantled long-term contracts and left pipelines with few options to open access.

8. The District of Columbia Court of Appeals remanded Order 436 for further rule making in 1987, but reaffirmed that the FERC had the power to impose open access status on interstate pipelines (*Associated Gas Distributors et al. v. FERC*, 824 F.2d 981 [D.C. Cir. 1987]). The intent of Order 436 was carried out in Order 500, issued in August 1987. Order 500 also contained a controversial crosscontract crediting scheme (See De Canio, 1990).

Chapter 2

Regulation versus Markets

Pipelines have long been considered to be natural monopolies and they have been regulated as the theory prescribes. The conclusion that pipelines are natural monopolies is based on certain core beliefs: that there are economies of scale in pipeline size and output, that duplicating pipelines would be wasteful, and that there is a need to plan the installation of pipelines and coordinate their operation to achieve the economies that are inherent in a network.

The argument for regulation says that it is best to have decisions and actions taken by a single organization whose span of control matches the problems of coordination and scale. The regulated monopoly is the institutional embodiment of this argument. The state is the central coordinator and planner and the regulated monopoly is its agent. If the argument is right, this hybrid organization, which is a mixture of state and monopoly, gives the right span of control to solve the coordination problem and the right size of the production unit to realize economies of scale. The other half of the argument for regulation is that competition, with its decentralized and individualistic actors could not effectively coordinate all the required decisions; in competition, it is said, there is no central place to collect the information and no mechanism for integrating it to plan and operate the system. There would be too much competition and wasteful duplication of facilities. There would be inefficient coordination among pipelines, excessive entry and exit, and volatile prices. Competition, it is argued, is the best arrangement for an industry producing a homogeneous product for which a relatively small scale of production is efficient; it is not suitable for pipelines.

This diagnosis is wrong and the prescription is faulty. One of our objectives in this chapter is to examine the argument from the perspective we have achieved in the course of this work. The argument is wrong on several key points: it fails to consider that a pipeline is an element in a network; it assumes that the pipeline is organized non-competitively; it misrepresents how coordination is achieved in a complex system; this theory of regulation also is at variance with how it works in practice. It also badly misrepresents how markets work and how institutions coordinate competitive behavior; that topic is the central concern of this book and is discussed in detail in chapters to follow. We close the argument by showing that, at a deeper level, the argument for regulation is the planning-versus-markets argument.

REGULATION IN THEORY

The theory behind the regulation of natural gas pipelines is a familiar one.[1] Pipelines are considered to be natural monopolies because there are economies of scale in their construction and operation up to limit which is sufficient to serve the largest markets. Costs are subadditive and one firm is enough to serve the market at least cost if its average cost is declining at an output sufficient to fill demand at a price that exceeds average cost. Two or more firms having the same costs would raise total cost by duplicating pipeline facilities. They would also reduce each other's output, which would raise average cost.

Scale

Increasing returns to scale is a justification for regulation on two grounds, according to the theory: to avoid or control monopoly power and to prevent duplication of capital and a loss of scale economies. To accomplish these ends, it is said that price must be regulated to prevent monopoly pricing and inefficient output. Moreover, entry must be prevented to prevent duplication and a division of output that loses economies of scale.

Coordination

A second theoretical reason given for regulation is to improve coordination in an industry where there are externalities. A network industry, like gas pipelines, could fail to realize the economies of coordination if each pipeline segment is independently owned and operated. Competition, the theory says, could not achieve the coordination needed to operate efficiently the network because each firm controls only a small part of it and cannot internalize the gains of coordination over the portion of the network where they occur. Full coordination might require that all the segments be owned and operated by a single firm, so that all the externalities are internalized inside the firm.[2] Since this would mean the firm would be a monopoly, the theory asserts that regulation is needed to prevent monopoly abuse. A corollary is that planning the network configuration is best left to a single company or regulator.

Commitment

Another aspect of the normative theory of regulation is related to commitment and opportunism. A pipeline is a fixed asset; so is the collection system feeding gas to it from producing wells, and so is the distribution system that sends gas from the pipeline to users. No part of the system can operate without the other and the value of the assets in each part depends on what every part does. Since these assets are specialized and have little value independent of the other components, there is a potential for each to hold up the others. If, after all the assets are in the ground, one segment opportunistically seizes on an unanticipated event or an ambiguity in the agreements to hold up the others, they cannot move their assets to another use. It may not be possible to write a contract that prevents all the possibilities for opportunistic actions. To prevent opportunism, the components could be merged, but that would give the merged firm too much power, according to this theory.

By supplying a tribunal for adjudicating these disputes and specifying rules of behavior, regulation might avoid the opportunism to which private contracting is susceptible. The theory asserts that regulation can supply a more secure and broader form of contracting than markets. By reducing the scope for opportunistic behavior, regulation can lower the required rate of return for specialized assets and permit a socially valuable project to go ahead. However, since the regulator holds no equity in the regulated firm, it bears no cost for taking opportunistic actions against it. The constraint that would bind is if the firm goes out of business. The contract theory would make more sense if the regulator had something at stake to limit its own opportunism.

The Regulatory Contract

The social contract theory of regulation broadens the scope of contracting beyond the pipelines to include customers. Customers are considered to be among the parties to the regulatory contract. The regulatory apparatus is, then, considered to be an institutional mechanism for social contracting among users, pipelines, and suppliers of natural gas. The testable propositions are harder to identify for this expanded theory, but they must include those already advanced above and go farther. It would imply that the terms available to every user are at least as good as a market would supply.

If this theory were true, regulators would not break contracts at all, and they would never break them with the frequency and audacity with which they have broken them in natural gas.[3]

FAULTS IN THE THEORY AND PRACTICE

Looking back over events and drawing on what we have learned in the course of research for this book, we want to point to some of the faults in the standard, normative theory of regulation.

Networks

The simple theory of economies of scale neglects important features of the industry. Producers and users are diverse. Their uses vary by type of transmission, by time, by season, and by location. Supply sources also are diverse and variable. Uncertainty and diversity can alter the simple picture given by the theory of scale economies, where output, cost, and demand are assumed to be known and certain. In this case, a more dispersed pattern of pipelines can be more efficient than a single, large pipeline. A network of smaller lines can connect to more points of supply and use to pool their variations and load patterns. A network can provide more paths between points and make it possible to alter routes to avoid capacity bottlenecks.

By focusing on a single pipeline, the natural monopoly argument misses a crucial point. To supply a flow of gas to a large line, one must have a large system of lines feeding the trunk line and similarly on the delivery end. Thus, in order to support the large flow that can realize economies of scale on the trunk line, one must have hub and spoke arrangements at the ends to supply and distribute the gas. This may be more costly than other arrangements such as three or more smaller trunk lines connecting more directly with supply basins and points of use.

Coordination

In order for economies of scale to be a real basis for a natural monopoly, the economies must be internal to the firm; that is, economies must be of such a scope that they can be captured only within a single firm and not by two or more firms. Where are the scale economies? Are they in planning or operations?

They cannot be in operations. One can hire a coordinator who will be efficient without exercising monopoly power. There is a competitive supply of coordinators (they might earn some information rents, but that is all). If they are not in operations, are there scale economies in planning? The theory would not claim that superior planning is a source of natural monopoly. It maintains the contrary, that a monopolist would undersize a pipeline rather than be a superior planner to competition. If a case can be made that natural monopoly is required for superior planning, it has to be on the grounds that the entire network of pipelines has to be under the control of a single planner.

But no one has ever tried to make the claim that all natural gas pipelines should be owned and operated by one firm. And this would not be a scale economy anyway; it would be a network economy, more like an economy of scope than an economy of scale. On these grounds, markets are demonstrably better at operating networks than regulated monopolies. At many points in the chapters that follow, we show that open access and markets transformed the pipeline grid, making it more connected and transforming it into a coordinated network. Before that, there was no network.

Centralized control is not clearly more effective than decentralized control once the system becomes large and complex. There is a confusion in the natural monopoly argument between coordination and allocation. To grant the authority to coordinate transportation on a pipeline does not grant the authority to allocate transportation among users. The two functions are separable. A good example is the procedure pipelines and shippers use to coordinate their monthly shipments. The shippers nominate the volumes they intend to ship. They must inject and withdraw gas according to the rules of operation of the pipeline and in accordance with their nominations. This achieves coordination of shipments and pipeline operations.

Pipeline Organization

The case for regulation rests on the particular organizational structure that the theory of natural monopoly assumes of the firm. By assuming that both the coordination and allocation of output are centralized under one authority, the theory forces the pipeline to be a *de jure* monopolist. The source of natural monopoly is the organization of the firm.

Regulation encouraged or even required centralized ownership and control of the pipeline. It discouraged vertical integration of the pipeline with gas producers and distributors. Federal legislation, in the Public Utility Holding Company Act, barred holding companies. These companies integrated horizontal segments of the pipeline grid and spanned wide geographic areas. They also were effective competitors to locally franchised gas utilities.

The monopoly problem in natural gas pipelines is an organizational problem, the consequence of combining and centralizing the authority to coordinate and allocate output in the hands of one agent. When the pipeline holds all of its transportation capacity, it considers the impact of each marginal unit of output on the price it receives for all units of output. It is this centralization of the output decision that causes the inefficiency usually attributed to monopoly. But, when units of capacity are owned by separate individuals, they compete with one another to supply transportation. The decentralized ownership structure that results from separate ownership eliminates the monopoly problem because each owner does not consider how his actions affect the prices received by other holders of capacity.

Natural monopoly is an unnatural organizational structure for decreasing cost activities and one that is seldom seen outside regulated industries. Examples where coordination and economies of scale are achieved without monopoly control can be found in many industries. These competitive forms of organization achieve economies of scale while decentralizing output decisions:[4]

- A water district can achieve the coordination required to solve the common pool problem. A hired coordinator monitors and enforces the mutually accepted appropriation rights of the members of the district. Coordination is achieved to solve the common pool problem, but control of the rights to allocate water is decentralized to the individual members who contract with the water district.[5]

- Taxi dispatch services are often supplied by a dispatcher hired by a cooperative formed by independent taxi operators. The economies of central coordination are gained by contracting while preserving a decentralized system of pricing and operation of cabs.

- Some oil pipelines are organized as joint ventures. Several shippers own fractional interests in the capacity of the pipeline in proportion to their equity in the firm. Together, they contract with a coordinator (often one of the co-owners) to balance and manage load and to monitor the users so no one exceeds their allocated capacity.

- A similar relationship is the joint ownership of a generator by several electric utilities which divide its output according to a formula that is related to their shares of ownership. A compatible division of the output and a monitor guarantees coordination among the owner/users.

- On large freight vessels, several shipping companies will own a fraction of the ship's capacity. Under these *space charter pacts*, shipping companies achieve economies of scale through centralized production, while the pricing and output decision of each capacity owner is decentralized.[6]

These cases show that economies of scale do not require a monopoly organization. Under a system where the ownership of capacity is decentralized, pipeline users have the ability to vertically connect segments on the line by acquiring the appropriate capacity rights. Horizontally integrated pipeline networks can be created through the acquisition of transmission rights on connecting lines. There is evidence that this might have been the solution the industry was inclined to take early on were it not for federal regulation and the Public Utility Holding Company Act.

Planning

Another claim made for regulated natural monopoly is that, as an organization, it is a superior planner to competition. This would say that the natural monopoly is guided by the regulator, who approves all projects and pricing. Since the regulator looks over all projects, he or she may be able to plan the system in a way that is superior to unregulated monopoly or competition. Planning means that the impact on the entire network is considered and that the future plays a part in approving projects. This theory does not stand up to the facts. The pipeline network never took form until deregulation and the emerging gas market transformed it. Before that, pipelines were separate and segmented because regulation blocked the formation of a connected network. As to the superior foresight of regulators, one need only point to the chaos and crises that drove the move to deregulate well-head prices and which is moving through every segment of the industry from the well head to users.

A source of planning inefficiency in regulated monopoly is that the regulated price of gas contains stale and irrelevant information, mostly about historical and sunk costs. The prices are not forward looking. Because future gas demands are unknown, expectations must be formed to guide decisions and there must be a stable basis for correcting error. Prices supply this information and the incentive for error correction is in profits. Regulators do not have the means to discover price and they blunt the incentives for error correction and adaptation.

There have been repeated and damaging shortages during which households went without heat and industries were shut down. The industry has been deep in litigious turmoil for many years. Furthermore, gas prices were unresponsive to market conditions and, at times, they were locked into a self-feeding cycle propelled by a perverse pricing mechanism to move out of step with, and even counter to, demand and supply. These events hardly sound like the result of good planning.

Wasteful Duplication

Another claim made for regulation is that it prevents wasteful duplication. The ironic aspect of this argument is how far from realizing the supposed benefits of preventing duplication we are under the present system of regulation. Intrastate and interstate pipelines duplicate one another to a significant degree. This is partly the fault of the artificial jurisdictional boundaries that carve regions into isolated protectorates. In nearly every local distribution area, there are private distribution systems operating in parallel with the public utility distribution company. One reason they do this is to get better terms and reliability than the local distributor can give them. Another is to cover parts of the region the distributor's system does not. Yet another is to augment the coverage where the distributor's coverage is inadequate.

But, it is important to get away from the mental picture of a pipeline or a distribution system as a single, fixed, and unchanging object that serves a single market. A pipeline, whether it is an interstate or an intrastate pipeline, is a part of a national network. A distribution system is another part of the web. They are all part of one system through which gas flows. Open access helps us to refine our thinking on this matter because it makes us more aware that gas can flow between points along many paths in the network.

Opening a new link in the network can affect the flow that reaches many points, not only the points on that link. We show in Chapter 4 how the paths in the network expand when a pipeline opens itself to transportation; the paths expand between all points, not just those on the line. Moreover, most new projects do not duplicate an existing line; they partly parallel the route and usually extend or redirect the route as well. Consequently, something new is added that was not there before. How, then, does one say that any pipeline, proposed or constructed, is a wasteful duplication? It no longer is just a simplistic check to see if there is already a line between two points, as the textbook version of the theory of regulation would have it.

The Regulatory Contract

The regulator blocks entry to protect its franchisee and to prevent duplication of facilities. The firm has no choice to walk away from the contract; as long as it stays in business, it must operate as the regulator says. The only exit it has from the contract is to go out of business or to take the service to another area. No outside suppliers compete for the contract; it is a long-term marriage that is not subject to outside challenges. The customers have no choice. They cannot seek out other sources of the service because no one else is permitted to supply it. The state contracts on their behalf and without their consent; these customers have to rely on the state to deliver the product and price it.

Consider how contracting and entry are interrelated. No firm enters a business like gas pipelines without having contracts assuring business to the entrant. Similarly, the incumbent firm has contracts with its clientele. Entry would only occur in such a situation if the prospective entrant can offer better contracts than the incumbent. So, the incumbent must meet the terms which potential entrants can supply. But, unless the customers are free to recontract (at the end of their terms or under an appropriate clause), outside challengers cannot improve the terms they can extract from the incumbent firm. The customers with the fewest options are hostages of the process; for them, there is no test of the proferred service against alternatives. If this were a real contract, the service would be voluntarily supplied and the customers would be free to choose it or some other service.

There is no need for entry to take place for competition to occur; in fact, the challenger would usually take the contracts and offer to sell them to the incumbent or buy the existing plant. No new construction is required at all. It is unnecessary to hold a state-run franchise competition to assure customers good terms and service. They simply must be free, at some point, to recontract with challengers to the publicly franchised firm. Public utility franchising does not permit this. Rather than barring wasteful duplication, it blunts the competition for customers and holds them hostage.

Rate Making and Hostages

Cost-based rate making loads risk on residential or so-called core customers that cannot be justified. Under cost of service rate making, core users are the residual source of funds to cover the mistakes or choices made by the other participants.[7] The obligation of the core to shoulder excess costs is the flaw in cost-based rate making. This is an obligation core users would not voluntarily take on, if they had any alternatives, and it is the first condition of the regulatory contract that ought to be reconsidered now that competition exists in natural gas.

Attempts on the part of the regulator to cross-subsidize the core through higher rates to other users only partly redress the burden. In order to cross-subsidize successfully, the regulator must set non-sustainable prices. To keep heavily priced users from leaving the system, their options must be cut off. Thus, making the core captive to the process also binds the other users. When other users opt out of the system to pursue competitively supplied services and escape the burden of cross-subsidization, cost-of-service rate making transfers the burden of the facilities they leave behind to the core. In addition, regulators require the system to be designed to assure delivery to the core at a level of assurance that is costly and which may exceed the reliability core users demand. The core has no economic means of expressing its demand for higher or lower levels of reliability. It is the core's vulnerability under cost-based rates that requires regulators to restrict the options of all users, core and non-core, for leaving the system.

Managing Complexity

The natural gas industry is complex. It is highly diverse and changing. The problem of regulating an industry is like the problem of running a socialist economy.[8] The planning and regulatory problems are information-processing problems: can the planner or regulator elicit and process the information required to direct an economy or an industry?

Hayek stated the issues in his famous debate with Lange over the possibility of a socialist economy—they could just as well have been debating the possibility of regulating an industry. His devastating criticisms of socialist planning and the collapse of socialist economies around the world caution us about the limited possibilities of well-functioning regulated industries.

In order to cope with the complexity of regulating the industry, regulators chose a classic approach to reduce a complex problem to manageability. They broke it down into smaller pieces. Congress, the Public Utility Holding Company Act, and the National Energy Act took over the organization of the industry and broke it into pieces with which regulators could deal. They carved off segments and handed them to the states, and they reorganized the industry to match jurisdictional boundaries.

By making pipelines and distributors into monopolies, they simplified the management problem. If there is only one firm to control and to be held accountable, regulation is much easier. Carving the industry into balkanized and isolated segments of monopoly both simplifies regulation and builds the need to protect.

Regulation shapes what sorts of information are processed. It controls the timeliness and level of information, what actions can be taken in response to it, and what incentives the parties have to respond to it. For example, price setting for pipeline tariffs is based on an allowed rate of return on assets. The information that goes into setting a price, say on segment k of a pipeline between nodes i and j of a network of pipelines linking many supply and use points at 4 p.m. on a Thursday afternoon in June is settled in a rate hearing that may have been held in November two years before. Furthermore, the rate was set, in part, on the basis of the cost of constructing the pipeline thirty-five years earlier. Almost no information specific to the time, place, and conditions on the relevant segment are used in pricing its use.

A regulatory agency that does central planning is an information bottleneck. There is no way that all the information out in the field can flow through the bottleneck, be processed, and orders returned to the field in a timely and accurate manner. Consequently, information about time and place must be ignored to lighten the regulator's information burden. Information must be pooled, averaged, segmented, and categorized according to regulatory authority. Distinctions and fine variations are made only in the rules and categories, not in the circumstances that make a difference in the operations in the field.

OTHER THEORIES OF REGULATION

There are other theories of regulation than the one we have discussed. They pose a less benign role for regulation than the strongly normative theory that remains the standard (it is popular with consultants and regulators, perhaps for the way it justifies their actions and fees).

One of the alternative theories of regulation is the protection theory. According to this theory, the decision to regulate and the way it is done stem from a desire of interest groups to protect the regulated firm. The interest group may be the industry as a whole, or it may be others, such as customer groups. By establishing a monopoly and closing entry two things are accomplished: the firm is protected and the protected monopoly can earn rents. These rents can go to the industry or they can be divided among the interest groups that promote the monopoly.

In reality, lobbying for monopoly is rare; what one sees is lobbying for controls of all sorts that have no clear overall impact on producers or anyone else. The protection theory does not deal with the surest aspect of regulation that we have discovered, that is, nobody really knows what they are doing. The unanticipated consequences of apparently simple regulations or changes can be staggering, and no one knows how to predict the impact. The protection theory has some ability to explain what we have seen of regulation, but it has no dynamic that would help us understand how the industry reeled from crisis to crisis since the 1970s and how the price control crisis triggered the unravelling of regulation and the rise of markets.

Regulation appears to be political control of the industry; it's not regulation in the classic sense at all. Like politics, what is done to the industry is hard to predict, and the complexity of the industry makes the outcome impossible to predict. Politicians want to control the industry for the power and control it gives them. They can trade legislation with their colleagues if they have an industry to control. Politicians are coalition builders who must respond to strong external changes in the environment to rebuild their coalitions in order to sustain their positions and functions. This may be hard to do at times, depending on the nature of the external shocks.

The political entities include the regulatory commissions and the Congress, which creates them. Together, they build coalitions representing themselves, users, suppliers, and all the other parts of the industry. The membership or participation constraints determine who is in and out and how far their gains of membership can be pushed before they leave. Each member must get from participation at least what he could get outside the coalition.

Of course, by not permitting exit, regulation can lessen the effect of these participation constraints. The core can have all its options removed, so that it cannot get out. Then the others can be bound to the coalition on the grounds that the core is the hostage. If the core is numerous, this strategy can work. But, overall, the core will not benefit because its options are removed by the process. Coalition members can be held close to their zero surplus level.

Given a complex system and a dynamic world, regulation can build a system of prices and services that becomes un-sustainable. We have seen this several times in natural gas. Agreements and contracts had to be undone, price regulation went through five regimes, and regulation spread from the user all the way back to the producers and then came apart. As in any sustainable coalition that achieves political control of an industry, the combined claims of the members, which reflect what they can get outside the coalition, must not exceed the total value of resources available to the coalition. When they do, the system must collapse. It then can only be rebuilt on a new, and reduced, set of claims and, maybe, with different members. By blocking exit and altering constraints, the system can be made to work for a time, but the complexity of the interlocking constraints means that they must frequently be violated. Then a fix is required, as in the many changes of regulatory regime that have been made to natural gas. However, do regulators understand what they are doing? In this complex problem, regulation is just a blind search for a sustainable coalition and not for efficiency.

It is difficult to explain what has happened in natural gas in any other terms. There were many other ways to build or structure the industry, but other systems would not have sustained the need for regulation in the way that the regulatory system has done in natural gas. What else explains the way the options of all the elements in the industry were cut off by regulation? How else can we account for the disastrous results of regulation and the success of markets?

A PREFERENCE FOR THE VISIBLE HAND

It is easier to build a case for regulation as control, and politicians have done so. They can draw on a western rationalist tradition that has a bias for control. We like to think we can design a good system and that it will work better than something that is unplanned and self-organized. If politicians can draw on a distrust for markets and a preference for control, they have a formidable base on which to build a case for regulation. They have a preference for the visible over the invisible hand.

Regulation was more than central control; it involved the active suppression of markets. It is based on the wrong idea of efficiency; it is a static efficiency that is strictly second order in magnitude. The whole standard theory of regulation is predicated on a static notion of efficiency; find the optimal output and set prices to support it, subject to non-negative profits. That presumes you know what you ought to produce and how and in what way production should be organized. It presumes all this information is known. It neglects entirely how this information is to be discovered.

Discovery takes experimentation and search over a broad landscape of alternatives. These are the things that promote first order efficiency because they help us decide what to do. Once we have decided upon a goal, the static optimization that is the basis for the standard theory of regulation might be worth pursuing, but only until the situation changes and new alternatives must be discovered.

At the bottom, the argument for regulation mistakes the origin of order. It does not come from conscious optimization and central control. It comes from noisy and recurrent non-linear feedback. This is to say, it comes from patterns borne of processes that reflect experimentation, learning, and adaptation; such systems evolve and adapt and are not frozen by a regulatory ruling. Evolution is not part of the regulatory design; that is its worst failing.

CONCLUSIONS

Between the theory of regulation and implementation of the congressional legislation is the requirement for the commission to make the process intelligible to itself and manageable. This means carving up and segmenting, separating, and finely defining. It means setting jurisdictional boundaries and creating all the definitions and procedures that have nothing to do with function. The gap between the Cartesian view of rational control and uncontrolled market forces is large. It is the gap in our understanding of self-organized complex systems and control that makes self-organization impossible.

Regulation made monopoly and created the conditions necessary to its own existence and survival. Without regulation, the industry would have been organized through joint ventures and vertical and horizontal integration. There would have been more holding companies to span and control segments over the network, and more shippers and users would be on the boards of pipelines. There would be less wasteful duplication of facilities. Most importantly, the industry would have preserved its ability to adapt to the challenges it had to meet.

NOTES

1. See Scherer (1980) or Kahn (1988).

2. This claim was made for the telecommunications network a decade ago by AT&T (Kahn, 1988). No one believes it now, if they believed it then.

3. Tussing and Barlow (1984) cite many examples of broken contracts up to 1984 and there have been more since. Smith, De Vany and Michaels (1988) argue that breaking contracts is a service regulators do for their clients.

4. These examples are drawn from the discussion of the role of regulation in De Vany and Walls (1994a).

5. See Smith (1988).

6. See Mahoney (1985).

7. Ellig (undated) cites the California Public Utilities Commission's frank admission that it fought new pipelines so that residential customers would not

end up paying for capacity that could be used to serve other markets. Why should they ever face this risk?

8. While the regulatory problem seems smaller than the planning problem, they are equally complex. The apparently simpler problem of regulation contains all the content of the seemingly larger problem of managing an economy. One can map every issue of the larger problem to the smaller one and vice versa, so they are equivalent—the regulatory problem contains all the complexity of the socialist planning problem.

Chapter 3

Crisis and the Emergence of Markets

In this chapter, we witness the emergence of a natural gas industry whose organization and function is based on markets. The rise of markets was made possible, and even required, by the massive failures of regulation. Markets wedged their way into the cracks of the crumbling regulatory edifice, and every new "fix" opened new opportunities for markets. None of this was planned and could not have been. After many years of regulation, it was not apparent where the problems or opportunities were. Each new group given access to a market in place of the old sources of supply and transmission seized the chance. Markets developed rapidly and everywhere they could; within five years of open access, there were more than fifty spot markets for natural gas and there was a rising chorus of users and suppliers calling for "bypass," the quaint industry term for getting around the barriers that regulators had put in the way of access to the market.

How these markets were organized and how they were linked together is the topic of this chapter. We focus on the institutional innovations needed to support natural gas spot markets and on the evolution of the network and its critical role in bringing these markets together. New market institutions had to be developed for trading gas; there were no such institutions under the old system. Prices are made in markets, not regulatory hearings, and they were being made in markets distant from one another. Gas trading is decentralized in markets scattered over the United States. Mechanisms for delivering access to transportation on open pipelines to users had to be put in place. Trading and shipping gas, often over routes that had not been used before, had to be coordinated by means that were compatible with operating requirements and flows in the network. The means for reporting and communicating trades, and the important price information which they contained, had to be developed.

The purpose of this institutional apparatus was to support the smooth operation of markets and the flow of gas over paths which markets, not regulators, dictated. This was a formidable institutional challenge for gas had never flowed in response to price signals before, or over the diverse routes now open. New kinds of contracts were devised to replace the long-term "take or pay" and "minimum purchase" deals that had dominated the industry.[1]

THE ELEMENTS OF CRISIS

Throughout most of the twentieth century the gas industry has adapted its behavior to an environment determined by government regulation. Markets were suppressed and were not part of the industry's basic institutions or ways of doing business. Everything turned on questions of regulatory approval and procedure, and the industry worked very badly. By the latter part of the 1970s, natural gas was the worst regulated industry in the United States. Shortages and curtailments were common and disastrous. Industries were shut down or their gas use was heavily restricted. Gas reserves reached a historic low relative to consumption. Regulation had not only lost control, it was causing the damage, and no hearing or resolution of a technical regulatory issue could restore the integrity of the gas supply system.[2]

The slow collapse of the industry and the potential for very serious gas shortages forced Congress to increase the industry's reliance on markets and diminish the scope and harm of regulation. But changes in the patchwork of regulation that had been built up over the fifty to seventy year history of government control of industry structure and operation began to pull the whole fabric apart. Congress and the FERC had to make many more changes to fix a cascading sequence of problems that had built up over the years and strained the system to the breaking point. It turned into an avalanche that swept aside much of the content of regulation, if not its apparatus.

Special Marketing Programs

By the time pipeline gas prices were nearing $10.00 per thousand cubic feet (MCF), there was gas to be sold for $1.50 per MCF and buyers willing to take it; but they could not execute the transaction. Why? The pipeline was the only intermediary. The solution was to bypass the pipeline. The pipeline owners would not want that, however, since they had contracted to buy at high prices the gas they were now trying to sell for $10.00, and they could not sell it if sellers and buyers could bypass the pipeline and deal directly with one another. To do that, they had to be able to transport the gas, which meant the pipeline had to carry it on their behalf, without being able to sell its own gas.

In 1983 Transcontinental Gas Pipe Line Company (Transco) struck a deal with its producers. They were not selling any gas anyway since almost no one was buying at the high prices. Transco would transport the gas for producers, who could sell it directly to buyers they could find, and the producer would credit that gas against Transco's obligation to buy from the producer. Everyone gained: the producer got to sell gas he could not sell otherwise, Transco got revenue from transporting the gas and relief from its contractual obligation to "take" gas at prices it could not pass on to buyers, and gas customers were able to purchase gas at rates substantially below the regulated rates available from Transco. This arrangement was called a special marketing program (SMP). It opened the way for a new organization for pipelines and for the whole industry.

Not everyone could take advantage of the SMPs as they were organized. The pipeline did not release all of its customers to the SMPs because, if it did, it would lose the revenue from its "core" or captive customers who could not switch to alternate fuels as readily as some of the pipeline's other customers. If the pipelines lost these customers to SMPs, they would lose most of their ability to recover the cost of the high-priced gas they had contracted for largely to supply this set of customers.

FERC Orders

The FERC ruled against minimum bill contracts. These were contracts between the pipeline and the distributor that supplied gas to the captive customers in its area.[3] By 1983 these contracts obligated the distributors to buy gas at prices that were far above the best prices available in the market, prices that were available to utilities and industrial customers who had the SMPs available to them for their gas purchases. In Order 380, the FERC abrogated minimum bill contracts and freed the distributors to buy gas anywhere. They had to find a way to get gas transported by pipelines whose owners were reluctant to do so. Pipelines believed they had contracted for the gas on behalf of the distributors, who ought to pay the bill.

This impasse was broken after Congress threatened to make pipelines common carriers. The FERC issued Order 436 giving the pipelines two choices: continue to operate as private carriers and live with take or pay obligations, or become contract carriers and get some relief from take or pay. Nearly all pipeline companies chose to become contract carriers within a year or two of the order, but the U.S. District Court voided Order 436 because it did not resolve the take or pay issue. The FERC also set forth Order 451, which would move well-head prices closer to, or above, the market price. This was the only gas the pipelines still had under contract at favorable prices.

THE TRANSITION TO CONTRACT CARRIAGE

In making the transition from merchant to contract carriage, the FERC required pipelines to permit customers who held firm purchase agreements to convert the callable volume to uninterruptible transmission rights. On making that election, the holder of transmission capacity is obligated to pay a reservation charge which depends only on the volume of gas for which uninterruptible transportation is reserved, and a volumetric charge for each unit of gas shipped. Most of the transmission capacity in the pipeline grid is under contract to the companies who distribute it in the city gate market to wholesale and retail customers. These local distribution companies were the major buyers of gas before open access, and they inherited transportation capacity when their gas contracts were converted to transportation contracts.

The FERC approved these transportation transactions individually until October 1985 when it issued Order 436 permitting interstate pipelines to transport gas for others under "blanket certificates." This order formally distinguished and separated the pipeline merchant and transportation functions.[4] After some initial skepticism, pipelines began to make application to become "open access" pipelines. As Table 3.1 shows, the number of pipeline applications and approvals for open access grew rapidly from 1985 to 1990. Within three years of Order 436, nearly all the major pipelines had become open access pipelines.

Between 1982 and 1987, transmission of pipeline-owned gas decreased 60 percent, while transmission of customer-owned gas increased by 180 percent.[5] Transportation accounted for two-thirds of all interstate gas movements by 1987, and in 1991 over 85 percent of gas shipped in interstate commerce was owned by customers.[6]

NEW MARKET INSTITUTIONS

Coordination

Pipelines coordinate their customers' transmission demands during what is called bidweek.[7] During the bidweek, usually the third week of each month, pipeline customers nominate the gas volumes they plan to ship during the following month. These nominations specify the injection point, the withdrawal point, and the volume of gas to be shipped. Customers may nominate volumes only up to the amount of their firm transmission rights. Those pipeline customers who transfer their transmission capacity to third parties are responsible for nominating and paying for it. The simultaneity of gas and interruptible transportation markets during the bidweek coordinates the purchase of gas and transportation. The spot contracts are for volumes to be delivered to specific injection points on the pipeline system. From the injection point, the

Table 3.1

Pipeline Application and Approval Dates for Open Access

Region	Pipeline	Application	Approval
West Texas	El Paso	6/88	11/88
West Texas	Transwestern	12/87	3/88
East Texas	NGPL	6/86	5/87
East Texas	Tennessee	12/86	6/87
East Texas	Trunkline	6/86	4/87
East Texas	Panhandle	6/86	11/87
North Texas	ANR	6/88	7/88
North Texas	NGPL	6/86	5/87
North Texas	Northern	6/86	1/88
South Texas	NGPL	6/86	5/87
South Texas	Tennessee	12/86	6/87
Louisiana	ANR	6/88	7/88
Louisiana	Columbia	12/85	2/86
Louisiana	Tennessee	12/86	6/87
Louisiana	Texas Gas	8/88	9/88
Louisiana	Trunkline	6/86	4/87
Louisiana	United	10/87	1/88
Oklahoma	ANR	6/88	7/88
Oklahoma	NGPL	6/86	5/87
Oklahoma	Northern	6/86	1/88

Source: U.S. Energy Information Administration (1989).

gas flows through the interruptible transmission right that is purchased in the bulletin board market to the downstream destination.

These institutions support a wide range of trading of transportation and natural gas over the vast network of pipelines that connect markets with supply basins.

Transmission

Holders of firm transportation contracts may trade with one another or transfer their rights to brokers and other parties. However, FERC has not permitted transportation to become a fully transferable property right.[8] Unused firm transmission capacity reverts to the pipeline, which sells it as interruptible transportation. Pipelines monitor throughput and post unused capacity for sale on electronic bulletin boards. These bulletin boards are accessible to all market participants who can buy interruptible transportation at the tariff posted by the pipeline. Because the tariffs may be discounted below the regulated tariff, the price of transportation adjusts continuously to clear the market, up to the maximum regulated tariff. In peak periods, the regulated tariff may become a binding upper limit on the market price of transportation.[9]

There are twenty-one major interstate pipelines and fourteen hundred local distributors who hold transportation contracts on those lines.[10] If they hold or acquire transportation contracts, gas users in each downstream market can purchase from all the fields to which they are directly or indirectly connected. If the prices across fields are disparate, gas purchasers will demand transportation connections to gain access to fields with low prices. Gas producers in fields with low prices will demand transportation connections to gain access to customers in downstream markets with high prices. When new pipeline interconnections are made, gas can flow to reduce price disparities anywhere in the network of interconnected pipelines.

All of the conditions needed to support gas trading have been met:

1. Brokers capable of transacting throughout the network have come into existence.

2. Mergers and interconnects have been made throughout the network.

3. Market institutions were created to coordinate gas and transportation trades.

Brokers buy and sell gas throughout the pipeline network, even though they do not have uninterruptible transmission rights of their own. They aggregate the supplies of producers and the demands of gas users. By purchasing interruptible transmission from the pipeline, they can ship gas from the producers to the users. Essentially, brokers hold a portfolio of gas market transactions which they match. Some brokers act as the purchasing agent for downstream local distribution companies. These brokers use the customer's transmission capacity to deliver the gas which they sell to the customer.

Pipeline mergers have created extended networks. The technology for interconnecting pipelines quickly developed after 1985, so that it is now possible to interconnect lines with different pressures and to change the flow between them.[11]

OPEN ACCESS AND MARKETS

Markets quickly came forth as pipelines chose open access status. A few years after Order 436, *Gas Daily* was reporting spot prices at over fifty markets and almost none of these had been active before Order 436. The volume of gas transported on behalf of customers rose rapidly, reaching 80 percent in just a few years, and it has remained above that level into the present.

The pace of open access applications and approvals was rapid. The first approval came in 1986, ten came in 1987, and another nine had been approved by the end of 1988. As open access spread through the pipeline network, spot markets opened at fields and interconnection points. The number of spot markets reporting prices to *Gas Daily* grew from zero in 1985 to nearly fifty by 1990. The growth in spot markets is evidenced in Figure 3.1, where it is apparent that the number of markets doubled from 1987 to 1990. By 1990 it was possible to make delivery throughout most of the pipeline network, and a natural gas futures market opened on the New York Mercantile Exchange (see Chapter 7 for more on the futures market and its role in pricing).

CONCLUSIONS

The long-term contracts which had organized the natural gas industry were unsustainable. Price shocks and price regulation together caused the contractual relations to unravel. Regulators attempted to alleviate the shortages they caused, but this led to further problems. Once the existing contracts and regulation became unsustainable in 1983, some of the major pipelines were on the verge of bankruptcy from their contractual purchase obligations. They had to sell gas and to do that they had to transport it to the customer. That was the beginning of contract or open access transportation. The accumulated constraints of merchant carriage and onerous regulation became unsustainable and adjustments had to be made everywhere. This could not be accomplished by augmenting existing regulation. The industry reconstructed itself in the wake of the final crisis. What were the tools of this reconstruction? They were contesting markets, intermediaries and brokers, futures contracts and

Figure 3.1
Spot Markets Reporting Prices in *Gas Daily*

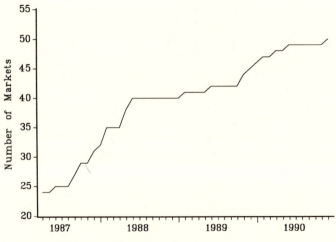

Source: De Vany and Walls (1994c).

markets, storage programs, tariff discounting, interconnects, arbitrage, lower prices, well-behaved prices, prices that contain valuable information (not the mix of ancient and stale rate hearing history), prices that guide decisions, hubs, and the emergence of a strongly connected interstate pipeline grid.

NOTES

1. Most previous research on natural gas markets has focused on long term contracts. See, for example, Masten and Crocker (1985), Mulherin (1986a, 1986b), Masten (1988), Hubbard and Weiner (1986, 1991), and De Canio and Frech (1993).

2. See MacAvoy and Pindyck (1975) for a detailed study of the effects of natural gas price regulation on supply.

3. This discussion follows the development of Tussing and Barlow (1984).

4. Earlier FERC orders had already dismantled long-term contracts and left pipelines with few options to open access.

5. See U.S. Energy Information Administration (1989), Cramer (1991), Walls (1992), and De Vany and Walls (1994c) for more details on the transition from merchant carriage to contract carriage.

6. See Federal Energy Regulatory Commission (1991).

7. The discussion of the market institutions follows closely De Vany and Walls (1994c).

8. See Smith, De Vany, and Michaels (1988, 1990), Alger (1990) and De Vany and Walls (1994a) for a more detailed discussion of gas pipeline regulatory reform.

9. Because the pipeline's tariff and its price of gas are regulated and not responsive to demands or capacity constraints, the market price of gas delivered at the maximum tariff may exceed the regulated system gas price of the pipeline in the peak winter heating period. The pipeline's system gas is adversely selected when it is less than the market price.

10. See Bradley (1991).

11. See *Oil and Gas Journal*, August 6, 1990, pp. 41–48.

Part II

The Evolution of Markets

Chapter 4

Markets and Networks

A necessary condition for the emergence of the natural gas spot market was the transformation of the vast web of separate and disconnected pipelines—which had been created by regulation—into a network.[1] All this was linked together through the emergence of a pipeline network that was connected and no longer balkanized into separate regions and pipelines. The implications of the emergence of a connected network are developed as the second major theme in this chapter. We want to show how the network took form after the FERC Open Access rulings. We develop measures of its openness and connectivity, and show how these measures of structure evolved over time.

Not only do we measure the degree of connectivity of the network, but we relate this to the spatial distribution of prices in the network. Because arbitrage requires open paths, the spatial distribution of prices is superposed on the connections in the grid. Where a path between markets is not open, those markets will not be as closely connected to the other markets in the network and their prices will reflect this. By looking at the spatial distribution of prices and its dynamics, we can infer where the grid is connected and where there are isolated components within the grid. Here we show why that is true according to the logic of markets; the empirical elaboration of that point will occupy us in several of the chapters to follow.

SUPPLY CHAINS IN THE NETWORK

At the dawn of open access, gas markets failed to exist. The industry was organized as a collection of geographically separated monopolies.

- A single pipeline linked a field and city gate.

- Entry was blocked.

- Transportation and gas were bundled.

Figure 4.1
A Simple Pipeline Network

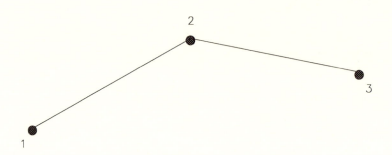

Source: De Vany and Walls (1994b).

- Gas buyers and sellers did not have access to one another.

- Gas purchases and supplies were made under long-term contract.

Open access was instrumental in transforming the rigid supply chains set in place by regulation. To see this, first consider the simple system shown in Figure 4 where point 1 is a field where gas is produced (a source) and points 2 and 3 are cities where gas is consumed (sinks). Under the regulated system of merchant carriage, gas could be transported from 1 to 2 and from 1 to 3, but not from 2 to 3. The pipeline was the sole buyer of gas at 1 and the sole seller at points 2 and 3. Entry was closed. We can represent this system by the accessibility matrix of its graph. The accessibility matrix captures the network structure of the space of possible transactions between points in the system. For the system shown in Figure 4, the accessibility matrix is a three-by-three matrix with a 1 where there is an edge connecting points and a 0 where there is no connecting edge. In the figure, there is a directed arc from point 1 to point 2. This is shown by a 1 in element (1,2) of the accessibility matrix. Since no flow may go from point 2 back against the flow of the line to the origin at point 1, the (2,1) element of the matrix is zero. Points 1 and 3 are similarly connected. Because only the pipeline sells gas, there are no possible trades between agents located at points 2 and 3 and so they are not connected. Each point is considered to be accessible to itself. The accessibility matrix of the space of transactions on the network of Figure 4 is:

$$
\begin{array}{ccc}
1 & 1 & 1 \\
0 & 1 & 0 \\
0 & 0 & 1
\end{array}
\tag{4.1}
$$

The significance of this regulated structure lies in three features:

- There is a single supplier at point 1—the pipeline as merchant selling gas bundled with transport. Gas buyers do not buy directly from suppliers, of which there are many.

- Gas buyers at points 2 and 3 cannot trade with one another: 2 cannot ship to 3 and 3 cannot sell gas at 2 even though it is flowing past 2 on the way to 3 (elements (2,3) and (3,2) are zero).

- Buyers at points 2 and 3 cannot resell the gas they buy from the pipeline back into the market at point 1 (elements (2,1) and (3,1) are zero).

The important features of open access and unbundling are those that transform these structural features of the transactions network to permit markets to be contested over a wider network. Consider how unbundling and open access change the accessibility matrix. Under open access the accessibility matrix becomes:

$$
\begin{array}{ccc}
1 & 1 & 1 \\
1 & 1 & 1 \\
1 & 1 & 1
\end{array}
\tag{4.2}
$$

The diagonal and first row of the matrix is the same as before open access: each point remains accessible to itself, and a user at either 2 or 3 can buy gas from a supplier at 1 and transport it to 2 or 3. The last term in the second row indicates that a trader can now take gas delivered to 2 and sell and deliver it to point 3. The first term of the second row represents a more complicated transaction: it indicates that gas can be sold from point 2 back to point 1, even though it is against the flow of the pipeline. This kind of trade may be called a "backhaul" or an "offset." It works because the gas that would be sent to point 2 can be delivered somewhere upstream of point 2 as a backhaul transaction, or it can be sold to another buyer in the producing area (point 1) as an offsetting trade or sale. Similarly, as row three of the accessibility matrix indicates, 3 can backhaul or offset transactions at 1, and 3 can sell gas at 2.

Not only is the space of transactions widened by open access, but the number of parties with whom one can transact is enlarged. Each buyer has access to every supplier at all the points in the network, including the original pipeline-merchant. The sparse accessibility matrix of the balkanized, regulated industry structure is contained in the open access accessibility matrix, which is populated by 1s everywhere in the network. This property of containment is crucial to our analysis for we analyze a sample of markets that becomes more deeply embedded in a network of markets over time; its matrix represents a small network of interconnected markets which is contained in a larger, sparse matrix which represents the national grid. Over time, the sub-matrix fills in with more 1s and the larger matrix becomes less sparse.

EVOLUTION OF NETWORK STRUCTURE

The spatial links over which gas can flow and trades can be made are represented by putting 1s or 0s in the appropriate rows and columns of the accessibility matrix. A network is connected if there is a path (a sequence of arcs) between all of its markets. A large network is connected if all of its sub-networks are connected and its degree of connection is roughly the number of its sub-networks that are connected.

The evolution of the pipeline network can then be characterized by the evolution of the accessibility matrix $A_t(\mathcal{N})$ that represents network $\mathcal{N}$ at time t. At the beginning of open access, when few pipelines were open, there are few 1s in $A_t(\mathcal{N})$. As more pipelines converted to transportation, the matrix becomes more dense with 1s. Components in the network become strongly connected and trading areas expand over a larger space.

The accessibility matrices evolve time $t = 0$ to time $t = T$ so that the following containment relationship holds:

$$A_{t=0}(\mathcal{N}) \subseteq A_{t=1}(\mathcal{N}) \subseteq \ldots \subseteq A_{t=T}(\mathcal{N}). \tag{4.3}$$

Each new matrix contains the old matrix as a subset because new links are opened and earlier links remain open. If, eventually, all pipelines open access to transportation, the network becomes fully connected and the accessibility matrix is filled in with all 1s. We use the following theorem from graph theory to compute the number of paths of various distances between the points in the network:

> The number of paths of distance $D_1, D_2, \ldots, D_{n-1} \leq D$ in the network $\mathcal{N}$ connecting markets i, j is given by the i, j-th entry in the $n \times n$ matrix $A^D(\mathcal{N})$.

In order to apply this theorem, we first derived the accessibility matrices of the pipeline system from maps of the transmission grid. Then we used these matrices and the theorem to compute the number of one-link and two-link

Figure 4.2
Paths of Lengths One and Two in 1986 and 1988 Networks

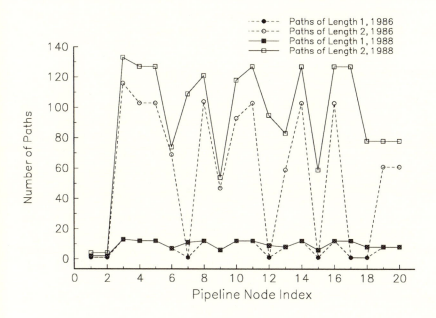

Source: De Vany and Walls (1994b).

paths connecting every pair of markets. The calculation was done for the network in 1986, an early point in the open access period, and in late 1988, after open access had been accepted by most of the major pipelines. The results are shown in Figure 4. The market points are numbered from 1 to 20 on the horizontal axis. The numbers of paths of length 1 and length 2 in 1986 and in late 1988 are on the vertical axis. For these purposes the number of points reachable by a path of length one represents all the paths from other markets to the market on the horizontal axis that use just one link in the transmission system; the number of paths between markets reachable by using two links are similarly defined.

In 1986 many of the twenty markets could be reached by a path one link long, meaning they lay within one open access pipeline connection to one of the other nineteen markets. By 1988 most markets could be reached by one link. The zero points on the graph indicate markets unreachable by length-one or length-two paths. By 1988 most pipelines were open and all but two markets could be reached by traversing any of fifty or more paths one or two links long from another market. The densely connected markets at locations 3 through 5 are pipeline hubs at highly connected components of the grid. These hubs are connected by over 120 paths to markets just two links away; that is why they became market centers.[2]

CONTESTING MARKETS IN A NETWORK

In addition to the more connected network which open access produced, another important feature is that the old story about barriers to entry is true no longer. In a connected network, gas suppliers can enter a market without constructing a new pipeline. They do it by purchasing short-term or interruptible transportation to supply gas to a market. The supplier can contest the market without making irreversible commitments. When temporary entry is no longer justified, the supplier can spin off transmission rights or stop buying interruptible transportation. "Hit and run" entry can occur when transportation is traded in an open market. As the transportation market develops liquidity, these costs will become lower. The ability to contest markets in this way represents a profound change from the situation that prevailed before open access—when entry and exit were severely constrained.

THE NETWORK LAW OF ONE PRICE

If there is a link and the cost of shipping or arbitraging gas is τ per unit, then prices in markets must lie within a distance τ of one another, namely, $d(p_1, p_2) \leq \tau$. If there is no link or if there are limits on the flow of the commodity over the link, then the prices can move farther away from one another, especially in short time periods. This is because it may take some time for a flow-restricted link to bring supplies to levels that bring prices back to arbitrage limits. Small flows may sustain equilibrium prices, but during transitions to new equilibria, a flow limit will delay price adjustment. In this case, prices may lie within a distance $d(p_1, p_2) \leq \tau + \omega(t)$, where $\omega(t)$ is a time-decaying function.

Suppose there are three points where prices are formed and that points 1 and 2 are indirectly connected by a path π_{132} through point 3. Then p_1 and p_2 are

$$d(p_1, p_2) \leq \min[\tau_{\pi_{12}}, \tau_{\pi_{123}}] \tag{4.4}$$

if neither path is at its capacity. If the capacities of both paths are required to move the flow, then

$$d(p_1, p_2) \leq \max[\tau_{\pi_{12}}, \tau_{\pi_{123}}]. \tag{4.5}$$

The arbitrage limits switch to their upper bound when there are bottlenecks on the flows, but over time the flow on the path dissipates so that the lower bound is reached. This illustrates some important features of prices in a network market: 1) prices are not unique; they are in an equilibrium set bounded by arbitrage limits; 2) the arbitrage bounds depend on the number paths and their capacities; 3) the arbitrage bounds depend on the flows on paths in the network and they can change when flows vary; 4) the flow dependence of arbitrage can delay the speed at which prices converge after at shock.

The points we made about price patterns in a network can be stated more rigorously as follows: Consider an $n \times n$ network $\mathcal{N}$ with markets and arcs (V, A). Let $\mathcal{P}(V, A)$ be the ordered set of equilibrium market prices, where we will use $p_j \in \mathcal{P}(V, A)$ to denote a typical demand price at j and $\rho_i \in \mathcal{P}(V, A)$ to denote a supply price at i. The arcs in the network are represented by a matrix, which we will denote as A in which every link is indicated by a 1 and missing links are indicated by a 0.

Shipping gas from i to j may involve more than one path in the network. When the tariff on each arc is given, the total cost of using the path $\pi \in \Pi_{ij}$ is $\sum_{a \in \pi} \tau_a$, where τ_a is the tariff on arc a of path π. There are alternate paths from i to j if the network is connected. A more strongly connected network on the same set of markets will contain more 1s and we treat the relationship of being more connected to be a containment relation in which a sparsely connected matrix is contained in a more strongly connected network (in the sense that changing 1s to 0s in the strongly connected network gives the sparsely connected one). A theorem of graph theory states that the number of paths $\pi \in \Pi_{ij}$ in $\mathcal{N}$ that are of distance $\leq D$ is the (i, j) element of the D power of the accessibility matrices of the network. Because the network is evolving over time, we index the accessibility matrices by time and then the following holds:

$$A_0^D(\mathcal{N}) \subseteq A_1^D(\mathcal{N}) \subseteq \ldots \subseteq A_T^D(\mathcal{N}). \tag{4.6}$$

Each new arc (a switch from 0 to 1) in the network creates new arbitrage paths that may expand at a power of the number of new arcs. Consequently, many new constraints are formed on prices whose arbitrage bounds are non-decreasing in the number of connected paths. Thus the sets of prices that are sustainable against arbitrage are ever more tightly bounded as the connection structure of the network evolves to higher connectivity over time:

$$\mathcal{P}(V, A_0) \supseteq \mathcal{P}(V, A_1) \supseteq \ldots \supseteq \mathcal{P}(V, A_T). \tag{4.7}$$

In the limit, this containment relation on prices goes to the competitive equilibrium. The supplies and demands are:

$$s_i = \sum_{\pi \in \Pi_{ij}} Q_\pi \tag{4.8}$$

and

$$d_j = \sum_{\pi \in \Pi_{ij}} Q_\pi, \tag{4.9}$$

where Q_π is the quantity flowing on path π. Since the buyer will obtain gas at the cheapest source, the condition on price is: For every market pair (i, j), $\forall j \in (V, A)$ and every path $\pi \in \Pi_{ij}$:

$$\rho_i = \min(p_j + \sum_{a \in \pi} \tau_j). \tag{4.10}$$

When the network is fully connected, these path constraints apply to all market pairs (i, j). For every market pair (i, j) and every path $\pi \in \Pi_{ij}$ the competitive equilibrium conditions obtain:

$$\rho_i + \sum_{a \in \pi} \tau_j \begin{cases} = p_j, & \text{if } Q_\pi > 0 \\ \geq p_j, & \text{if } Q_\pi = 0. \end{cases} \tag{4.11}$$

MODELING PRICES

In an earlier work we developed a model that maps connection structure to the spatial distribution of prices.[3] We denote the *change* in price at market i between time $t-1$ and t as $\triangle p_{i,t}$. Further, let ϵ_t be a white noise process that may be contemporaneously correlated across markets, and let W_t represent an exogenous factor that affects prices at each market.[4] Let $l \in [1, L]$ denote the temporal lag of a variable. The geographic and temporal structure of price changes can be modeled with the following equation system.

$$\triangle p_{1,t} = \omega_1 W_t + \gamma_{1,1,0} + \sum_{l=1}^{L} \sum_{j=1}^{N} \gamma_{1,j,l} \triangle p_{j,t-l} + \epsilon_{1,t}$$

$$\vdots$$

$$\triangle p_{i,t} = \omega_2 W_t + \gamma_{2,2,0} + \sum_{l=1}^{L} \sum_{j=1}^{N} \gamma_{i,j,l} \triangle p_{j,t-l} + \epsilon_{i,t} \tag{4.12}$$

$$\vdots$$

$$\triangle p_{N,t} = \omega_N W_t + \gamma_{N,N,0} + \sum_{l=1}^{L} \sum_{j=1}^{N} \gamma_{N,j,l} \triangle p_{j,t-l} + \epsilon_{N,t}$$

The sign and magnitude of $\gamma_{i,j,l}$ is an indication of the information which past price changes at other markets in the network contain about the expected price change at market i. If $\gamma_{i,j,l} \neq 0$ then the past price change at market j at time $t - l$ predicts the current price change at market i. Such a value of $\gamma_{i,j,l}$ would indicate an arbitrage opportunity either across markets, across time periods, or both. For example, if $\gamma_{2,6,1}$ were positive, then the price change at market 2 can be predicted from last period's price change at market 6. A trader could exploit this information by buying at market 2 whenever the price at 6 increases and the same point extends to all pairs of markets and time lags for which $\gamma_{i,j,l} > 0$.

The network law of one price states that $\gamma_{i,j,l} = 0$ for all i, j, l where there exist arbitrage paths. This is a law of arbitrage over points and time periods; it states that the price at each market incorporates the information contained in past prices at all the other markets to which it is linked by arbitrage paths. We define a path to exist between time periods whenever there is a link in the network. This simply reflects the fact that storage, or futures contracts, can be used to arbitrage between time periods between connected points. When points are connected, their prices can be arbitraged between the present and the future, and we say there are temporal arbitrage paths between periods whenever there is a physical path between the points in the network.

Equation (4.12) is a vector autoregression (VAR) model of the vector time series of prices at N markets. The empirical model characterizes the joint distribution of the data without placing external constraints on the price dynamics. The model contains $N^2 \times L + N$ coefficients which are to be estimated. Each coefficient corresponds to the information which the price at each location and prior time period contains about the price at a market in the network. The coefficients also correspond to potential arbitrage transactions; a coefficient which is different from zero indicates that prices corresponding to the non-zero coefficients contain information that can be used to make a potentially profitable arbitrage transaction.

Testing the law of one price is equivalent to testing the joint hypothesis that all the elements of the $N \times (N \times L + 1)$ matrix Γ corresponding to equation (4.12) are equal to zero. This joint hypothesis can be tested as an exclusion restriction; the likelihood ratio test statistic can be computed directly from the log determinant of the covariance matrices. Let T be the number of observations, r be the number of restrictions, and let Σ_R and Σ_U represent the covariance matrices for the restricted and unrestricted models, respectively. The likelihood ratio test statistic is distributed chi-squared with r degrees of freedom and is computed from the log determinants of the estimated residual covariance matrices as:

$$\chi^2(r) = T \left(\ln |\Sigma_R| - \ln |\Sigma_U| \right). \tag{4.13}$$

Since the null hypothesis is that the law of one price holds, a large value of the test statistic would lead to rejection of the law of one price.

MODELING MARKET INTEGRATION

We have chosen cointegration techniques to further examine natural gas prices because of their power in dealing with two key features of the gas market: it is a network of spot markets, and its prices vary over time.[5] Because gas prices are volatile, it is difficult to determine if prices at different points in the network lie within the bounds that competition would imply. Competitive prices at points in the network must be free of arbitrage opportunities, but within these limits they are free to vary with respect to one another. Thus, we must test two price series for arbitrage when they may be non-stationary and arbitrage only limits the range of volatility which they may exhibit with respect to one another.

Cointegration provides a way to test for arbitrage-free pricing in time-varying series. Two non-stationary series are cointegrated if they have a linear combination that is stationary. When p_i and p_j are each integrated of order one and cointegrated, their linear combination $p_{j,t} - \alpha - \beta p_{i,t} = \mu_t$ is stationary. If two price series are within stable arbitrage limits, the "spread" between them will be stationary and they will be cointegrated. Cointegration, therefore, is the natural test for market integration of stochastically varying prices.

Unit Roots and Pricing

Consider a time series of prices p_t and its autoregressive representation where μ_t is a Gaussian disturbance term, ρ is an autoregressive parameter, and t represents time:

$$p_t = \rho p_{t-1} + \mu_t. \tag{4.14}$$

This price series is stationary if the autoregressive parameter ρ is less than one in absolute value.[6] If $\rho = 1$, then the series has a *unit root* and its variance, $t\sigma^2$, becomes infinite with time.[7] If $\rho = 1$, Box and Jenkins define the autoregressive process generating p_t to be *integrated* of order one, $I(1)$.[8] In general, a time series of data is said to be integrated of order d if it must be differenced d times to make the series stationary.

Now consider two series of prices, p_i and p_j. Each series itself is non-stationary and must be differenced d times and b times, respectively, to achieve stationarity. However, there may be a linear transformation of the two original series,

$$p_{j,t} - \alpha - \beta p_{i,t} = \mu_t \tag{4.15}$$

that results in a series μ_t that is integrated of order $d - b$. If such a linear transformation between p_i and p_j exists, they are said to be cointegrated of order (d, b).[9] The non-stationarity in one series effectively cancels out a portion of the non-stationarity in the other. The cointegrating parameter is given in the "cointegrating regression" shown above as equation (4.15). When p_i and

p_j are each integrated of order 1, $I(1)$, and they are cointegrated, their linear combination μ_t will be stationary or $I(0)$. This case with $d = b = 1$ has been studied in the literature and is the relevant case for the empirical work in this book.[10]

Perfect market integration requires that the estimated cointegrating parameter $\hat{\beta}$ in the cointegrating regression be equal to one. Here the cointegrating regression specifies the no-arbitrage equilibrium condition. The constant α reflects the cost of transmission between market i and market j. When the price at market i increases by one unit and the cost of transmission remains constant, the price at market j should rise by an equal amount for the equilibrium to be restored.

Representation

Both of the preceding models of spatial pricing, arbitrage, and market integration are elements of a more general framework. Our general point is that the spatial distribution of prices in a network is determined by an adaptive pricing process, one that represents arbitrage, the connection structure of the network, and the distribution of shocks to points in the network. Our models are part of a modeling framework that is suited to the adaptive dynamics of arbitrage pricing in a complex network. This framework is a representation of an error correction model of the following form:[11]

$$\triangle X_t = \gamma + \sum_{i=1}^{k-1} \Gamma_i \triangle X_{t-i} + \Pi X_{t-k} + \mu_t \tag{4.16}$$

where X_t is an $p \times 1$ vector of prices that are integrated of order one, $\triangle$ is the difference operator, γ is vector of constants, and μ_t is a vector of Gaussian disturbances. The general adaptive model has two fundamental components: the so-called vector autoregressive component Γ_i and a cointegration component Π. Together these components represent aspects of a very general adaptive pricing model that places few restrictions on the data and permit us to capture the dynamics of prices and the relationships that hold over prices in the network. In our empirical analyses of pricing over different components of the natural gas market, we will employ vector autoregression and cointegration techniques as appropriate.

CONCLUSIONS

The theory of network pricing that we have presented in this chapter does place restrictions on the model. In the ensuing chapters we will see how the evidence and the theory match up and what the results tell us about the degree to which the gas market is integrated or segmented. We will also see how market integration relates to the connection structure and openness of access through points and links in the network.

NOTES

1. The material in this chapter follows and extends our earlier work on network connectivity and price convergence (De Vany and Walls, 1994b).

2. Commissioner Branko Terzic, in the report of FERC Pipeline Competition Task Force on Competition in Natural Gas Transportation identifies market centers as keys to competition in gas and transportation (Federal Energy Regulatory Commission, 1993).

3. See De Vany and Walls (1994b).

4. In the econometric model, the exogenous factor can affect the price at each market by a different amount.

5. See De Vany and Walls (1993) and Walls (1992, 1994a, 1994b, 1995) for more detailed discussion of applying cointegration techniques to quantify the strength of competition in a network.

6. See Harvey (1981).

7. The variance of each individual price series is unbounded because $Var[p_t] = t \times \sigma^2$ where $t = 1, 2, \ldots, \infty$ and σ^2 is the standard error of the white noise disturbance.

8. See Box and Jenkins (1970).

9. See Engle and Granger (1987).

10. If the arbitrage bounds are non-stationary, the price series may be cointegrated of a higher order. For example, suppose that the arbitrage bounds were $I(2)$, that p_1 were $I(3)$ and p_2 were $I(1)$. In this case the linear combination of p_1 and p_2 is not stationary even if the series are cointegrated; it would be $I(2)$ if the pressure of arbitrage caused the prices not to diverge from one another. In general, the difference in the order of integration of the two series must equal the order of integration of the arbitrage bounds.

11. See Engle and Granger (1987).

Chapter 5

Markets in the Producing Areas

In this chapter, we trace the evolution of spot markets in the production areas. Our concern is with understanding how the spatial distribution and dynamics of prices evolved as these markets progressively were embedded in a larger web of open pipelines and interconnected markets. One important factor in this evolution was the emergence of "market centers" for gas and transportation trading at the places where pipelines intersect or pass so close to one another that a short link is all that is needed to connect them. These centers connect the network and make possible the flexible routing of gas that allows shippers to contest many markets from any supply point. Another crucial factor was the attainment of a connection structure that opened enough paths in the network to arbitrage that the segmented spatial markets underwent a transition to an integrated market.

As always in this book, our focus is on pricing in the network. In this chapter, that translates into a concern for how the market mechanism and pricing are affected by the connection structure of the network. Is the network sufficiently open so that supplies in every market on the network can be pooled against price changes in other markets? Have the regionally segmented markets set in place under regulation become integrated? Does the spatial distribution of prices look as though the markets are integrated? At what time in the evolution of the network did this happen? Do prices have good dynamics over the network?

A FIRST LOOK AT PRICES IN FIVE REGIONS

Before we proceed to the more formal analysis, it is interesting to see how the spatial distribution of prices evolved over time. Let us examine regional spot prices which cover the time frame from the earliest period of open access, 1984, and end in 1993. The spot prices in five regions are plotted in Figure 5.1. The pattern of prices appears to have changed over time. There are three distinct patterns: in 1984–1985 regional prices move independently, in 1986–1987 there is a period of increased volatility and prices move together, by 1989 the series move in step with one another, and they begin to drift within a narrower band by 1992. For all regions, the standard deviations of the price spreads decline from 1984–1985 to 1988–1989.[1] The spreads increase in the winter months because pipelines become congested and do not discount their tariffs.

SPATIAL PRICING IN THE NETWORK

As the connections increase in the network, the set of prices that can be sustained against competition from other markets becomes more compact (this was shown in the preceding chapter). Because of uncertainty and transactions cost, the constraints that other markets impose on the price at any given market define a set of prices, not a unique equilibrium price. If prices at each node reflect all information in the network at each point in time, and all arbitrage possibilities have been fully exploited, then the price of gas at each node on a given day should be the best predictor of the following day's price. If tariffs are stationary, then price changes should approximate a white noise process. Otherwise, there will be profitable opportunities for trading over the network. Wherever there are paths between markets on the network, price disparities between them cannot persist.

This "no arbitrage possibilities" idea can be made more explicit by drawing on the model of Chapter 4 to represent the price at each market as a function of the previous day's price at that market and exogenous factors. There are two dimensions along which to test the hypothesis of no exploitable arbitrage possibilities: over time and across the network. For the hypothesis not to be rejected, the first differences in prices at each node in the network cannot depend on the past price differences for that node, nor for any other node. This means that the equations must be expanded to include the across network arbitrage as well as temporal arbitrage.

THE NETWORK PRICE DATA

Gas Daily reports prices at over fifty pipeline interconnection points. The interconnections are where smaller pipelines feed gas from the producing fields to major pipelines, or where major pipelines meet. Our sample includes twenty markets for which *Gas Daily* reported prices since 1987. It was important to have markets that were open long enough to see how their pricing relationships evolved with the network. The markets are located in six geographic regions: West Texas, East Texas, North Texas, South Texas, Oklahoma, and

Figure 5.1
Natural Gas Spot Prices by Region

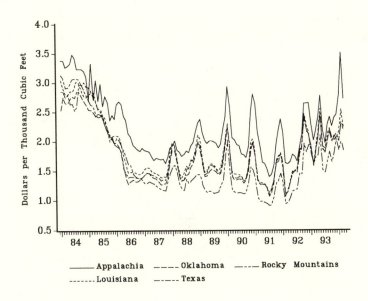

Source: Energy Information Administration.

the Louisiana Onshore region. Table 5.2 gives the opening dates of the pipeline systems where these markets are established. We know when these markets opened and where they are located; moreover, we know how they are connected to pipelines and other markets.

The daily spot prices are a weighted average of each day's trades. These prices are for gas injected into the pipeline at the market for which the price is listed. The prices include all gathering and transportation fees incurred to get the gas to the points for which prices are reported. All prices are based on dry packages of five million cubic feet per day stated in dollars per million Btu ($/MMBtu) for spot contracts of thirty days or less.

We partitioned the data into three equal sub-samples: July 1987 to June 1988, July 1988 to June 1989, and July 1989 to June 1990. The data are segmented in this way so that each period begins and ends in an off-peak period, and so that we can evaluate changes in the model's estimates and convergence properties over the interval from July 1987 to June 1990. Prices were tested for non-stationarity. These test results indicate that the price series are integrated of order one and not greater than one.

PRICE RELATIONSHIPS

The vector autoregression model of equation (4.12) was estimated for six different networks. We were unable to include all of the nodes in the regression at one time because the number of parameters to be estimated increases rapidly with the number of markets included in the network. By looking at several networks, we can determine if and how opening the pipeline network led to a convergence in prices across locations and pipelines. What follows is a description of these networks and a discussion of the test results.

The first two networks, listed in Table 5.1 as Networks 1 and 2, contained a market from each of the six areas. These networks differ in structure. In Network 1, the markets are on different pipelines in each region. In Network 2, four of the markets are on the same pipeline (NGPL) and two nodes are on other pipelines. This means Network 2 is more highly connected than Network 1. The cost of inter-lining a shipment of gas between pipeline systems might affect prices. Network 3 includes all of the markets in East Texas and Louisiana. Network 5 contains all of the markets in Oklahoma and North Texas. These networks span large areas and each contains 252 unique arbitrage possibilities. Networks 4 and 6 contain markets within a particular region.

For the July 1987 to June 1988 sub-sample, the hypothesis of a fully arbitraged network is rejected for each of the six network topologies. There were opportunities for arbitrage during this period. For the period from July 1988 to June 1989, the no arbitrage hypothesis is rejected for all of the networks except Network 6. This is the network containing five pipelines in Oklahoma.

Table 5.1
Field-Field No Arbitrage Opportunities Test

Injection Nodes	Regions	1987–88	1988–89	1989–90	1990–91	$\chi^2(.05)$
Network 1						
El Paso	West Texas					
Trunkline	East Texas					
Panhandle	North Texas	268.40	192.80	84.53	309.50	134.35
NGPL	South Texas					
Tennessee	Louisiana					
Northern	Oklahoma					
Network 2						
El Paso	West Texas					
NGPL	East Texas					
NGPL	North Texas	256.05	232.29	11.60	126.69	134.35
NGPL	South Texas					
Tennessee	Louisiana					
NGPL	Oklahoma					
Network 3						
NGPL	East Texas					
Tennessee	East Texas					
Trunkline	East Texas					
ANR	Louisiana					
Columbia	Louisiana	468.75	427.36	402.72	189.48	290.02
Tennessee	Louisiana					
Texas Gas	Louisiana					
Trunkline	Louisiana					
United	Louisiana					
Network 4						
ANR	Louisiana					
Columbia	Louisiana					
Tennessee	Louisiana	193.08	192.39	110.45	101.69	134.35
Texas Gas	Louisiana					
Trunkline	Louisiana					
United	Louisiana					
Network 5						
ANR	Oklahoma					
Northern	Oklahoma					
NGPL	Oklahoma					
Oklahoma	Oklahoma					
Panhandle	Oklahoma	565.09	455.60	N.A.*	N.A.*	290.02
ANR	North Texas					
Northern	North Texas					
NGPL	North Texas					
PEPL	North Texas					

(Table 5.1 *continued*)

Injection Nodes	Regions	1987–88	1988–89	1989–90	1990–91	$\chi^2(.05)$
Network 6						
ANR	Oklahoma					
Northern	Oklahoma					
NGPL	Oklahoma	127.53	99.27	46.11	52.11	101.85
Oklahoma	Oklahoma					
Panhandle	Oklahoma					
Network 7						
ANR	North Texas					
Northern	North Texas					
NGPL	North Texas	218.64	78.22	90.95	45.65	69.83
PEPL	North Texas					

* Denotes that model was inestimable due to singularity of the data matrix.

This network was tightly connected and its prices indicate its markets were integrated. For the period 1989–1990, the model could not be estimated for Network 5 because the data matrix was singular. The "no arbitrage" hypothesis was rejected for Network 3. Most importantly, the hypothesis of no arbitrage could not be rejected for any of the other networks. That means Networks 1, 2, 4, and 6 were, by 1989, strongly connected and had prices that reflected this fact. As we have seen, by this time most pipelines had opened their systems to transportation. Hence, the pipeline network appears to have achieved a "critical" level of connectedness by 1989.

PRICE DYNAMICS

To explore the dynamic behavior of the spatial distribution of prices, we calculated impulse response functions for Network 1 for each of the time period samples.[2] Using estimates of the spatial and temporal pricing model for Network 1, we increased the price at an arbitrary market (the impulse) and then traced out the responses of prices at the other markets in the network. We trace out the path of prices at each market for $t = 1, 2, \ldots$ time periods, assuming that no further exogenous shocks occur. The graphs of the impulse responses show the dynamic behavior of prices in the pipeline network.

Simulating the path of prices by shocking a single price may be misleading when all of the price series tend to move together. To account for the historical (contemporaneous) correlation in the residuals, they are made orthogonal to one another by use of the Choleski factorization, which is the standard method.[3]

Figure 5.2
Price Propagation across Network 1, 1987–1988
Price Responses on the El Paso Pipeline in West Texas

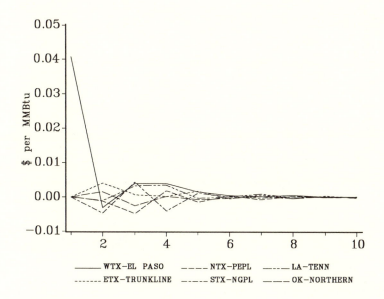

Figures 5.2, 5.3 and 5.4 show the impulse response functions on Network 1 for each sub-sample: 1987–1988, 1988–1989, and 1989–1990. The response functions show the response of the price on the El Paso Pipeline in West Texas in response to exogenous shocks to prices at all pipeline nodes contained in Network 1.[4] Comparing these impulse response functions, one can see the dramatic change in the speed and range of price convergence over the three time periods. In the 1987–1988 period, it takes six or seven trading days for prices to converge. In the 1987–1989 sub-sample, prices converge more rapidly and paths are less volatile. By 1989–1990, price shocks are absorbed within a day or two.

COINTEGRATION RESULTS

The data were segmented into four one-year samples to make comparisons between years possible. Our reasons for looking at different time periods are to

Figure 5.3
Price Propagation across Network 1, 1988–1989
Price Responses on the El Paso Pipeline in West Texas

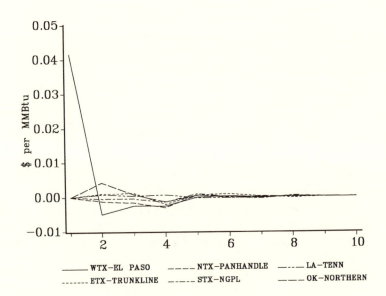

Figure 5.4
Price Propagation across Network 1, 1989–1990
Price Responses on the El Paso Pipeline in West Texas

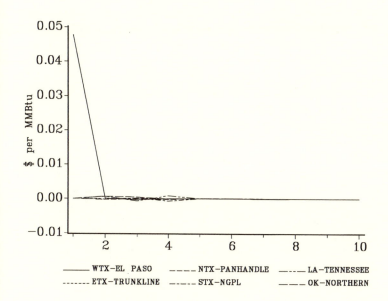

see if the spread of open access pipelines and the development of new markets and pipeline connections over time succeeded in linking gas markets more tightly.[5]

Each sample begins in July and ends the following June.[6] Each price series was tested for non-stationarity using the Dickey-Fuller test and the Augmented Dickey Fuller test with four lags. Since we know each individual price series is non-stationary, we proceed to see if there is a linear combination of pairs of price series that is stationary. Even though the individual price series may diverge (have infinite variance), the prices should not diverge from one another if they are constrained by arbitrage limits. We created a matrix of market-pairs from our sample of 20 price series. Every market was paired with every other market, giving a matrix of 190 ($20 \times 19/2$) unique market-pairs to test for cointegration. In those markets that are linked by arbitrage, the differences between their price series should be stationary, which means they should be cointegrated since each price series is $I(1)$.

Cointegrating regressions were estimated by ordinary least squares for each of the 190 market-pairs for each of the four periods 1987–1988, 1988–1989, 1989–1990, and 1990–1991. The regression equations take the form of equation (4.15).[7] In 1987–1988, 87 (46%) of the 190 market pairs showed evidence of cointegration at a marginal significance level of 5 percent. In the following year, 103 (54%) of the market-pairs were cointegrated. This figure rose to 124 (65%) in 1989–1990 and 126 (66%) in 1990–1991. The cointegration test results are summarized in Table 5.2.

The increase in the number of market-pairs that are cointegrated is evidence that markets became more integrated over our sample period. An example of this is the West Texas region. Four market-pairs in the West Texas region served by El Paso and Transwestern pipelines were cointegrated in 1987–1988. By 1989–1990, the West Texas region was integrated with thirty-two other markets. By 1991 this high degree of integration lessened to a degree, primarily on the Transwestern pipeline. However, during the same period South Texas, North Texas, and Oklahoma became more integrated with other markets. The market integration statistic for nearly all market-pairs drifts upward over the entire sample period, and this increase can be interpreted to indicate that most pairs became more strongly cointegrated. By the end of the sample in 1991, the degree of cointegration between distant market-pairs approaches the cointegration of near pairs.

INTERPRETATION

Some markets are better integrated than others. As was noted earlier, transitory breaks in the arbitrage-pricing inequality may occur due to binding capacity constraints along some pipelines. As more pipelines became open

Table 5.2
Number of Spot Prices Moving with a Particular Spot Price

Region	Cointegrated 1986-87	Cointegrated 1990-91	Application	Approval
WTX-El Paso	4	17	6/88	11/88
WTX-TRANSW	1	15	12/87	3/88
ETX-NGPL	14	12	6/86	5/87
ETX-TENN	14	16	12/86	6/87
ETX-TRUNK	11	11	6/86	4/87
ETX-PEPL	10	13	6/86	11/87
NTX-ANR	1	1	6/88	7/88
NTX-NGPL	12	17	6/86	5/87
NTX-NORTH	4	16	6/86	1/88
STX-NGPL	5	14	6/86	5/87
STX-TENN	0	14	12/86	6/87
LA-ANR	15	10	6/88	7/88
LA-COLUMB	13	13	12/85	2/86
LA-TENN	11	14	12/86	6/87
LA-TEXGAS	14	15	8/88	9/88
LA-TRUNK	10	13	6/86	4/87
LA-UNITED	13	13	10/87	1/88
OK-ANR	13	1	6/88	7/88
OK-NGPL	12	13	6/86	5/87
OK-NORTH	5	7	6/86	1/88

Source: De Vany and Walls (1993).

access, the number of routes and the transmission capacity between origin-destination pairs increased. Thus, the price series become more strongly cointegrated as open access expands through the network because the arbitrage-pricing inequality is violated less frequently by hitting capacity constraints. Moreover, open access expands the number of arbitrage paths, promoting a tighter arbitrage-pricing inequality.

One way to explore this connection between cointegration and the open access status of pipelines is to see with how many other regions a region's price is cointegrated relative to its open access date. Table 5.2 presents this information; for each pipeline and region it indicates with how many other points that pipeline's price is cointegrated. For example, the first two rows show that there are two spot prices in the West Texas region, one at the El Paso Pipeline injection point and the other at the Transwestern Gas Pipeline, and it indicates that spot prices at these points were cointegrated with 4 and 1 other points in 1986–1987 and 17 and 15 points in 1990–1991 for El Paso and Transwestern respectively.[8]

The first fact that stands out in this table is that open access came unevenly over the regions, beginning with applications dated as early as December 1985 and as late as June 1988. Approvals began to be granted by the FERC as early as February 1986 and ending as late as November 1988. By late 1988, all the regions in the sample were connected via an open access pipeline. Even before applications for open access were approved, all of the pipelines had interim transportation programs that supported limited spot market trading. The reliability of these spot markets was not assured until the open access application was approved and until trading grew to a level that would give the market the depth required to assure it as a reliable source of gas. Wider participation and widening access to points in the network went hand in hand in the development of the spot market.

By the last sample period, all the supply regions are connected to more than one open access pipeline: West Texas—2, East Texas—4, North Texas—3, South Texas—2, Louisiana—6, Oklahoma—3. The degree of cointegration of a region with other regions is not related to the number of pipelines connecting the region to the national market. For example, West Texas has but two pipelines and yet WTX-El Paso and WTX-TRANSW prices are cointegrated with seventeen and fifteen of the nineteen other markets with which they could be cointegrated. With the exception of one pipeline—ANR—every pipeline-regional price is cointegrated with at least as many other regions in 1991 as it was in 1987. When the level of integration is high in the 1986–1987 sample, that region's open access date occurs during that time period. When the level of integration increased from 1986–1987 to 1990–1991, the open access date of the region is after 1986–1987 and before 1990–1991. Thus, the increase in the number of cointegrated regions from 1987 to 1990 coincided with the opening of access in those regions during that time period.

CONCLUSIONS

Our empirical examination of natural gas spot prices in twenty spatially separated markets leads us to conclude that gas markets became more strongly integrated from 1986–1987 to 1991. We tested each daily price series for 190 market-pairs representing arbitrage points in the national pipeline network. The price series were non-stationary and follow a random walk. Early in the sample, soon after open access became an effective policy, only 46 percent of the market-pairs were cointegrated. By 1991, 66 percent of the market pairs were cointegrated and the degree of cointegration became independent of the distance between the pairs. The spread of open access through the grid was not uniform, and the pattern of cointegration shows discontinuities that match the opening of key pipelines. Open access has provided the basis for integrating separate and even distant gas markets into one market. Policy should aim at removing the remaining barriers to pipeline integration.

NOTES

1. See De Vany and Walls (1992, 1994c).
2. See Lütkepohl (1991, pp. 43–59) for a detailed discussion and exposition of impulse response analysis in multivariate time series models.
3. A drawback of the Choleski factorization is that it differs for each ordering of the variables, so the impulse response functions will also differ; we computed the impulse responses for several orderings of the variables and found that our qualitative conclusions were unaffected. As an alternative to the Choleski factor, the residual covariance matrix could also be factored by an eigen decomposition or a Bernanke-Sims structural decomposition. Theory offered no compelling restrictions to place on the residual covariances, so the structural decomposition method was not pursued.
4. The impulse response functions can also be computed for the other five pipeline nodes contained in Network 1. We do not display them here since they contain essentially the same information as is contained in Figures 5.2, 5.3 and 5.4. See Appendix C of Walls (1992, pp. 142–150) for graphs of all of the impulse responses.
5. Open access and markets spread rapidly during the sample periods. In 1987 about ten open access applications submitted to the FERC had been approved. By 1989 about twenty-seven applications representing nearly all of the major pipelines had been approved. During the same period the number of markets reporting spot prices doubled from about twenty-four to fifty. See De Vany and Walls (1994c).
6. MacKinnon's (1990) Monte Carlo generated critical values were used for all of the unit root and cointegration tests. Earlier studies used Dickey and

Fuller's critical values or Engle and Granger's critical values. MacKinnon has constructed a manifold of critical values for a continuum of sample sizes; these critical values are programmed into MicroTSP.

7. Results similar to those reported here were obtained using the Augmented Dickey-Fuller test and a lag selection criterion. As suggested by Engle and Yoo (1987), a formal lag selection criterion was used to determine the number of lagged residuals to include in the testing equations. The lag selection criteria of Akaike (1973) and Schwarz (1978) each indicated lag lengths not greater than four, so four lagged residuals were included in the ADF testing equation. This lag length assured that the residuals from the testing equation were white noise.

8. The application and approval dates were compiled by Doane and Spulber (1992) from Energy Information Administration documents and FERC sources.

Chapter 6

City Gates

We saw in the last chapter that most, though not all, markets in production fields and hubs are integrated. Most customers who use gas are not located at the production fields: they are far from the fields and behind a city gate where gas must be transferred from the interstate long-haul pipeline to a local distribution system. If a user cannot move the gas over an interstate pipeline and into a local distribution system and, finally, to a point where it is actually used, then the competitive field market is unreachable and possibly of little benefit. In this chapter our focus shifts from the production areas to the city gates. We follow the gas as it moves beyond the production area and pipeline pooling centers to the city gates. We ask how closely prices at the city gates are linked with prices in the production fields and pipeline hubs. We shall see that a few city gates are well integrated with the production area markets; however, most are not as well integrated as they could be if the city gates were completely open access.

As in the previous chapter, our focus is on pricing in the network. In this chapter, that translates into a concern for how the city gates are connected to the network and open to arbitrage paths. The primary question we seek to answer is: Are the local delivery systems and the gate between the local distribution system and the interstate network sufficiently open so that spot prices at city gates are subject to the same kind of arbitrage forces that we found at work between the production areas and pipeline hubs?

THE INTERSTATE LEG

A user can buy gas at any market in a field or a hub. However, such a buyer must have some assurance that the gas can be carried over the interstate pipeline to the point of entry into the local distribution system that will be used to make local delivery. We have already shown how the interstate leg of the trip from field to city gate can be accomplished under the evolving rules of

Open Access. Under the curious arrangements created by regulators, the same organization that controls the local distribution system behind the city gate also controls the firm transportation capacity that links the fields to the city gate; the organization is the local distribution company. This is so because the capacity of interstate pipeline systems is vested in the local distribution companies that held firm contracts for delivery through the interstate pipeline before Open Access began.

As we discussed in Chapter 2, the vesting of interstate transportation in the hands of local distribution companies was part of the arrangement made in the Federal Energy Regulatory Commission's Order 436. In Order 636, the distribution companies were granted more flexibility in transferring the firm capacity they inherited, and were obligated to pay for, to others. As a result, interstate transportation has become a resource that can be reallocated among potential users. The interruptible transportation that the pipelines inherit— from users who fail to exercise all their firm transportation rights—is sold in a bulletin board style market that is maintained by each pipeline. The bottom line is that if you want to transport from a production area to a city gate, you have to make arrangements to use firm capacity that is held by a local distributor at the city gate where you demand access; otherwise you have to settle for interruptible transportation which may be purchased in the bulletin board market. All of these factors limit or condition access over the interstate segment to the city gate and make it less likely that markets located at city gates will be as well connected as the production fields and market centers that are tied together over the interstate network.

GETTING THROUGH THE CITY GATE

The city gate is the terminus of the interstate trunk pipeline and it is the point where the gas carried on the long-haul pipeline must be injected into the local distribution system. The gas might "bypass" the local distributor if the customer has a private pipeline network to receive and distribute gas to the locations of use. For example, large utilities and industrial users often have their own facilities for bypassing the local distributor. Most gas buyers, however, are not able to bypass local distribution directly and must rely on transmission through the local distribution system to deliver the gas from the city gate to the point of use. If these buyers cannot gain access to move their gas through the local distribution grid, then their ability to make gas deals in the fields and use open access to transport gas over the long-haul pipeline will be insufficient to get the gas to their point of use. Open access on the long-haul interstate pipeline may offer no benefits to customers behind the local distributor's city gate if the gate is closed and locked.

Some gas distributors have opened their systems to marketers and others for local transmission. When access to the local system is open, a marketer can buy gas in the field, ship it to the city gate over a long-haul open access pipeline, and then inject the gas into the local system for delivery to end users. This transaction "bypasses" the local distributor *qua* gas merchant, even though it uses the distributor as a transporter of gas. Another transaction that achieves the same result is to buy the gas from a supplier who has delivered it to the city gate and then inject it into the local system for delivery to the buyer's burner tip.

Most local regulators do not permit the gas distributors under their jurisdiction to implement a system of open access, although this reality is rapidly changing. In this respect, local regulation is at odds with federal regulation, which encourages open access. For example, current regulations do not allow gas users within California to transact directly in gas and transportation markets. However, the Southern California Gas Company (SoCalGas) has implemented a form of open access through their "Targeted Sales Program." This program allows customers to buy upstream gas and transport it through the SoCalGas distribution system; the program implements open access while conforming to strictures of the local regulatory body, the California Public Utilities Commission.

In the program, gas users make their deals directly with producers. After a deal is made, the buyer calls the gas distributor to have it formally make the purchase at the terms agreed to by the gas seller. The gas distributor takes title to the gas at the city gate and then delivers it to the buyer's point of use. The gas buyer then reimburses the gas distributor for the purchase price of the gas and pays a transmission fee.[1]

Core customers have also gained access to producers. Direct purchases from producers can be delivered to core customers through what is known as the "Core Aggregation Program." A broker wishing to sell to core customers behind the California city gate can aggregate the demands of core customers. The broker can then buy gas from a producer on the spot market and arrange for its transportation through acquisition of long-haul transmission rights on the interstate pipelines.[2] The local transportation is arranged with the local distribution company the same way it is done in the Targeted Sales Program. In Southern California, this pilot program is allowed to serve 10 percent of the core market, creating competition for the core market that once was considered to be the local distribution company's captive market.

Now many other city gates are open to some form of bypass. Lyon and Toman (1991) report that by 1988, 88 percent of local distribution companies had established a transportation service on behalf of customers who purchased gas for themselves. About 22 percent of the gas delivered by these local distribution companies was owned by the customer. The conversion of interstate pipelines from merchants that transported their own gas to contract carriers that transport gas for their customers and the opening of the city gates to bypass have fundamentally changed the network structure of the gas market. It now is far more connected than under the balkanized structure that was created by regulation. Are there enough arbitrage paths to bring these points into the national field and hub market, or are they still limited and a little out of step with production area prices?

ARBITRAGE

Arbitrage can exert an influence on prices only if there is a path over which the commodity can flow to bring prices within arbitrage limits. If a city gate is to be open to arbitrage, then there must be paths that go through the city gate to users on one end and sellers far away in the fields at the other end. If there is a link and the cost of shipping or arbitraging is τ per unit of gas, then the prices in the two markets must lie within a distance τ of one another, namely, $d(p_1, p_2) \leq \tau$. If there is no link, or if there are limits on the flow of the commodity over the link, then the prices can move farther away from one another, especially in short time periods. This range of prices results because it may take some time for a flow-restricted link to bring supplies to levels that force prices to lie within the arbitrage limits. Small flows may sustain equilibrium prices, but during transitions to new equilibria, a flow limit will delay price adjustment. In this case, prices may lie within a distance $d(p_1, p_2) \leq \tau + \omega(t)$, where $\omega(t)$ is a time decaying function.

If there are two or more links whose capacity is necessary to sustain the flows that both serve and arbitrage the markets, then prices will lie in an interval $d(p_1, p_2) \leq \max \text{ or } \min[\tau_\pi, \forall \pi \in \Pi_{ij}]$. This inequality means that the arbitrage limits switch to their upper bound when there are bottlenecks on the flows. But over time, the flow on the path will dissipate and the lower bound may be reached. In the long run, if there is enough capacity to handle the flow on one path, the minimum bound will hold. Several important features of prices at city gates follow from this simple analysis: 1) prices lie in an equilibrium set bounded by arbitrage limits; 2) the arbitrage bounds depend on the openness of the gate—the number and capacities of paths that go through it to production areas; 3) the price limits depend on the flows through the city gate and along the paths in the production areas so that price bounds widen when capacity bottlenecks are binding; and 4) arbitrage bands change dynamically with flows so that prices can show time dependence in the transition to a new equilibrium.

TESTING SPATIAL ARBITRAGE AT CITY GATES

The field markets we use are located on four pipeline systems that connect six geographic regions—West Texas, East Texas, South Texas, North Texas, Oklahoma, and South Louisiana—to cities and to one another. The sample includes six city gates and three critical vertices where many paths in the network are connected; these are the so-called hubs where market centers emerged. The data are daily spot prices at city gates and hubs for 1990 through 1991 from *Gas Daily*. The prices are for gas injected into a pipeline at the location for which the price is listed in Table 6.1. The prices account for the quality of the gas, since they are quoted as dollars per unit of thermal energy ($/MMBtu).

The matrix Γ of the vector autoregression model of equation (4.12) was estimated for several sub-networks in the national pipeline system. Preliminary estimates showed that lag lengths longer than three were insignificant, so the number of lag terms in Γ were set to three. The five networks over which the network law of one price was tested are shown in Table 6.1. The likelihood ratio test statistics are included in the table. The networks will be discussed in the order in which they appear in the table.

Network 1 contains the California city gate and producing areas in West Texas. The city gate is served by two interstate pipelines, El Paso and Transwestern, that connect it to the fields supplying gas to the West Texas pooling hub. Even though both pipelines end at the California city gate, they receive gas from different fields in West Texas, so there are three points where prices are formed and three spatial arbitrage paths connecting them directly or indirectly. Since each of these physical paths has three time lags associated with prices, there are, in all, thirty distinct physical and temporal arbitrage paths, where lags are included.[3] For this network, the law of one price cannot be rejected.

Network 2 is formed by enlarging Network 1 to include another pipeline, NGPL, that collects gas from fields located in North Texas. In this network, which contains fifty-two arbitrage paths, the law of one price is rejected. The gas injected into the NGPL at North Texas is headed for Chicago and other points north of Texas. Since NGPL has no direct connection to the California city gate, the North Texas gas that is injected into the pipeline cannot be shipped to Southern California. Yet, even in this larger network, prices between the four points converge within several days. Table 6.2 lists the arbitrage directions that individually are significantly different from zero at the 5 percent level. Four out of five of the arbitrage violations involve transactions across locations that are not physically connected by arbitrage paths. One of the other rejections is in the existence of a positive autocorrelation of prices at the California city gate; this is the only market to exhibit temporal dependence in its own prices. This dependence is consistent with the lag pattern

Table 6.1
City Gate Law of One Price Test Results

Injection Nodes	Regions	Test Statistic	5% Critical Value
1. California City Gate			
El Paso	West Texas		
Transwestern	West Texas	24.53	43.77
2. California City Gate			
El Paso	West Texas		
Transwestern	West Texas	80.88	69.83
NGPL	North Texas		
3. Chicago City Gate			
NGPL	North Texas		
Tennessee	Louisiana	53.97	69.83
NGPL	Oklahoma		
4. Chicago City Gate			
NGPL	East Texas		
NGPL	North Texas		
Tennessee	Louisiana	114.78	101.85
NGPL	Oklahoma		
5. California and Chicago City Gates			
El Paso	West Texas		
NGPL	North Texas	237.48	69.83

(Table 6.1 *continued*)

Injection Nodes	Regions	Test Statistic	5% Critical Value
6. Seattle City Gate			
NGPL	North Texas		
NGPL	Oklahoma	63.19	43.77
7. Seattle City Gate			
NGPL	North Texas		
NGPL	Oklahoma	92.78	69.83
NGPL	East Texas		
8. Northern TBS			
NGPL	North Texas		
NGPL	Oklahoma	41.15	69.83
NGPL	East Texas		
9. Maumee, Ohio			
NGPL	North Texas		
Tennessee	Louisiana		
NGPL	Oklahoma	100.13	134.35
NGPL	East Texas		
NGPL	South Texas		
10. Broad Run, West Virginia			
NGPL	North Texas		
Tennessee	Louisiana		
NGPL	Oklahoma	128.66	134.35
NGPL	East Texas		
NGPL	South Texas		

that the theoretical model showed could happen in a capacity-constrained market (more on this below).

Network 3 contains the Chicago city gate and two pipelines, the NGPL and Tennessee; these two lines serve fields in North Texas, Louisiana, and Oklahoma. There are fifty-two arbitrage paths in Network 3, counting time lags as paths. The law of one price cannot be rejected for this network. There

Table 6.2

Arbitrage Directions ($\gamma_{i,j,l}$) Significant at the 5 Percent Level

Network 2

i/j	California CG	El Paso	Transwestern	NGPL
California CG	$l = 1$	—	—	$l = 1$
El Paso	—	—	—	—
Transwestern	—	—	—	—
NGPL	$l = 1$	$l = 1$	$l = 3$	—

Network 5

i/j	California CG	Chicago CG	El Paso	NGPL
California CG	$l = 1, 2, 3$	$l = 1, 2$	$l = 1, 3$	$l = 1, 3$
Chicago CG	—	—	—	$l = 1$
El Paso	$l = 1$	—	$l = 1$	$l = 2$
NGPL	$l = 1$	$l = 1$	$l = 1$	—

is no arbitrage possible between the upstream and downstream Oklahoma and Texas injection points on the NGPL pipeline, nor can one arbitrage Louisiana gas going to Chicago on the Tennessee pipeline against gas going to Chicago on the NGPL from Oklahoma or Texas. Since both pipelines end in Chicago, they supply gas to the same market and their delivered prices cannot differ. Yet both pipelines undoubtedly have different rate bases and approved tariffs.[4]

Network 4 extends Network 3 beyond Chicago to include East Texas points that also supply Chicago. These East Texas fields connect to Chicago *via* the NGPL line, yet adding them to the network causes the law of one price to be rejected. There are eighty paths in this network and, in order to not reject the law of one price, the coefficients for all the paths must jointly be equal to zero. Analysis of the coefficients and simulations reported below show that price convergence in this network takes place within three days. This means arbitrage opportunities do exist from time to time, but they are eliminated quickly. Rejection of the law of one price occurs only on one path—the price change on the Tennessee pipeline in Louisiana predicts the spot price change on the NGPL line in North Texas three days hence.

Network 5 deliberately contains city gates that are not directly connected to one another. Network 5 contains the California and Chicago city gates, two pipelines, El Paso and NGPL, and two production markets that lie between them, West Texas and North Texas. In this network the law of one price is rejected more soundly than in the other networks. It is not possible to ship gas from Chicago to California, so why should one expect their prices to be linked tightly? The answer is that, with open access transportation on the El Paso and NGPL pipelines, if California's price rises out of line with Chicago's, a trader could buy gas in West Texas for delivery on the El Paso pipeline to California and sell the same amount in North Texas where NGPL takes gas for delivery to Chicago. In a network, price disparities at the city gates can be traded away at the fields or interconnection pools. Table 6.2 lists the γ coefficients that individually are different from zero at a 5 percent marginal significance level. Of the sixteen significant gamma coefficients, twelve of them involve transactions across points that are not connected.

The rest of the violations of the law of one price have primarily to do with the fairly high autocorrelation of prices at the Southern California city gate, which we have already seen. If there is any city gate where arbitrage is capacity-constrained, our evidence says it is Southern California. Until recently, this area was served by two major pipelines and had a past history of gas curtailments. The Kern County pipeline has since opened to supply the northern portion of Southern California and another to bring gas from Canada is in hearings.

Networks 6 and 7 contain the Seattle city gate and for each of these the law of one price is soundly rejected. However, none of the γ coefficients is individually different from zero at the 5 percent level even though all of the γ are jointly different from zero at the 5 percent level.

PIPELINE HUBS

One point of very great interest in the development of the natural gas spot market has been the emergence of the so-called hub areas as market centers. The hubs are points where several pipeline systems intersect in a radial pattern of spokes around the hub. The significance of these hubs is that pipelines are close enough to be connected readily by adding short links. This proximity means that a few new links can increase connections in the network and greatly expand the number of arbitrage paths.[5] Hence, the hubs are the points in the network where the largest number of paths between markets exist, and it is natural that the market centers should form first there.

Because of the critical role which the hubs have played in the emergence of a national gas market, we considered networks that are connected at hubs. These networks do not include city gates; they contain only producing fields and hubs. We consider three networks centered on the Northern Town Border Station; Maumee, Ohio; and Broad Run, West Virginia. The network law of one price test statistics are given for these as Networks 8, 9, and 10 in Table 6.1.

The Northern Town Border Station (TBS) hub is where Canadian natural gas enters the United States and it is a pipeline hub. In spite of its great distance from the Texas and Oklahoma production fields connected to it *via* the NGPL, the TBS price meets the law of one price with all these points. The two other pooling points, at Maumee, Ohio and Broad Run, West Virginia, are locations where gas from many fields converges on pipeline interconnections. For each of these pooling points there are 114 arbitrage paths (time and pipe included). The law of one price holds in these networks.

ANOTHER LOOK

De Vany and Walls (1993), Walls (1994), and others have argued that cointegration is the appropriate empirical method to use when testing the strength of market linkages with non-stationary data. Even if individual price series are non-stationary, their deviations from one another may be limited by geographic arbitrage, that is, the prices may be cointegrated.[6] When the price series are cointegrated, it is appropriate to model their joint determination through an error correction mechanism. The intuition of the error correction formulation is that economic forces will prevent persistent deviations from equilibrium conditions; deviations or errors from the long-run equilibrium at time t will cause prices to converge toward their long-run relationship in subsequent time periods. If the production field and city gate prices are cointegrated, then competitive forces in the network must cause these prices to converge after they are shocked away from equilibrium.

The city gate price series is tested here for cointegration using the procedure suggested by Engle and Granger.[7] We estimate a bivariate linear regression using the price series in two cities and test the residuals for non-stationarity. Each price series was tested for non-stationarity using the Augmented Dickey Fuller test with one and four lags. The null hypothesis of a unit root could not be rejected for any of the field or city price series. The first difference of each price series $(p_t - p_{t-1})$ was also tested for a unit root and non-stationary was rejected, that is, the first difference of each price series is stationary. This is strong evidence that the price series follow a first-order autoregressive process.

Each of the 120 city gate-pairs in the sample was tested for cointegration using the Engle-Granger procedure.[8] Table 6.3 lists the Augmented Dickey-Fuller t-statistics for the cointegration tests.[9] The hypothesis that they are not cointegrated was rejected in 38 (32%) of the 120 city gate/field market-pairs and could not be rejected in the remaining 82 (68%) market-pairs at the 5 percent marginal significance level. This means that 38 of 120 market-pairs show price behavior that is stable and bound within stationary arbitrage limits. These results stand in some contrast to what we found in our preceding analysis of arbitrage and price changes.

Table 6.3
City Gate-Field Market Cointegration Test Results
Augmented Dickey-Fuller _t_-statistics

Field Market	City Market					
	Broadrun	California	Chicago	Maumee	TBS	Seattle
WTX-ELPASO	−3.284	−6.400*	−4.074*	−1.939	−2.698	−1.884
WTX-TRANSW	−3.143	−2.616	−2.612	−1.315	−2.361	−2.468
ETX-NGPL	−2.556	−4.312*	−4.327*	−0.618	−1.946	−3.826*
ETX-TENN	−3.139	−3.775*	−3.675*	−1.201	−2.484	−1.736
ETX-TRUNK	−2.384	−3.313	−3.777*	−0.867	−2.498	−1.939
NTX-ANR	−2.255	−2.745	−4.174*	−1.160	−3.503*	−3.236
NTX-NGPL	−3.850*	−4.023*	−5.306*	−1.955	−2.861	−3.487*
NTX-NORTH	−3.181	−5.184*	−4.220*	−1.547	−2.876	−2.853
NTX-PEPL	−3.247	−3.814*	−3.813*	−0.911	−2.758	−2.758
STX-NGPL	−3.006	−4.107*	−4.443*	−0.932	−2.174	−3.806*
STX-TENN	−2.711	−4.107*	−3.488*	−0.989	−2.287	−2.013
LA-ANR	−1.845	−2.936	−3.722*	−1.211	−2.826	−1.898
LA-COLUMB	−2.408	−3.403*	−3.825*	−0.954	−2.737	−1.836
LA-TENN	−3.741*	−3.597*	−3.596*	−1.479	−2.777	−2.049
LA-TEXGAS	−2.782	−3.317	−3.954*	−0.886	−2.646	−1.944
LA-TRUNK	−2.772	−3.201	−4.118*	−1.051	−2.683	−2.058
LA-UNITED	−2.135	−3.128	−3.874*	−1.216	−2.362	−0.857
OK-ANR	−2.215	−2.769	−4.056*	−1.063	−3.410*	−3.136
OK-NGPL	−2.884	−3.587*	−3.877*	−1.343	−2.322	−2.664
OK-NORTH	−2.811	−4.659*	−3.924*	−1.166	−2.538	−2.850

* Denotes that the null hypothesis of non-cointegration can be rejected at the 5% level. MacKinnon Critical Values for the null hypothesis of non-cointegration are: (1%) −3.937; (5%) −3.360; (10%) −3.062. At the 5 percent marginal significance level the aggregate results are: Reject 38 (32%) and Not Reject 82 (68%).

Source: Walls (1994c).

The Chicago city market is cointegrated with all of the field markets except the one located on the Transwestern pipeline in West Texas; it lies at the heart of a large cluster of pipelines and can receive gas from many directions and fields. We know that its city gate is open and its cointegration with the network suggests that there are enough open paths to production fields for arbitrage to work. The California city gate price is cointegrated with prices at twelve of the twenty field markets; the local gas distributor's access and bypass programs may explain why this is so. Nonetheless, as the evidence of price changes we developed in the previous section also indicates, the California city gate is not open enough to integrate its market into the production market. In contrast, the remaining city gate markets appear to be integrated with very few of the field markets.

ARBITRAGE IN ACTION

How quickly does the network restore prices? To see arbitrage and price convergence in action, we computed the impulse response functions for Network 1 and Network 5 using the estimates of the vector autoregression model.[10] The following experiment was conducted for each subsample. The price at an arbitrary point in the network was increased (the impulse) and then the responses were traced out for prices at each node.[11] The path of prices is traced for each node for $t = 1, 2, \ldots$, assuming that no further exogenous shocks occur. The graphs of these impulse responses show the convergence dynamics of prices in the network.[12]

The paths of prices at the California city gate after price shocks at three other points in Network 1 are shown in Figure 6.1. The price shocks are damped immediately, with no overshooting. In contrast, the price shocks in Network 5, shown in Figure 6.2, persist for up to seven trading periods after the initial shock. Even in this case, the variation in prices at different points in the network is small—they are within one cent of one another by the second day.

The experiments show that these networks absorb shocks readily and are homeostatic or self-correcting. City-gate markets need have little fear that their prices will be too strongly influenced by local conditions, perhaps with the exception of the capacity-constrained Southern California city gate. Local volatility is quickly damped by the network and its links to the pool of gas throughout its points of supply. A price shock in California sends a signal that redirects the flow of gas throughout the network to damp the impact, and this is true for other city gates.

Figure 6.1
Price Convergence across a Small Network

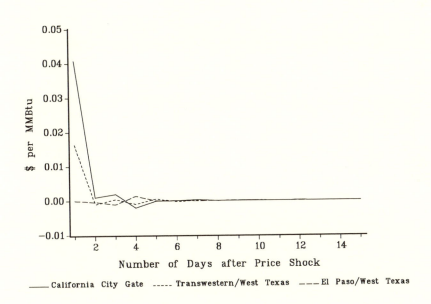

Figure 6.2
Price Convergence across a Large Network

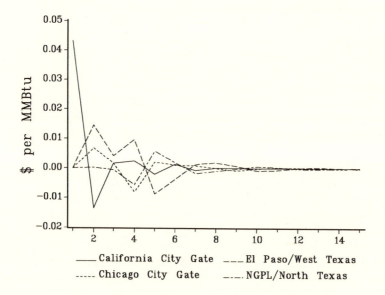

CONCLUSIONS

Open access pipeline transportation and partial bypass at the city gate have brought prices at most, but not all, city gates into line with prices in the fields. Chicago city gate prices track production area prices closely. Prices at the Seattle city gate do not track field prices very well. California prices track production areas reasonably well, but they do show price dynamics that indicate the presence of a capacity bottleneck. Price convergence at the city gates is not as rapid as convergence at the fields. Yet, open access is far from complete at the city gates and it shows in our evidence. Price changes do track one another closely, but they move outside arbitrage bands in capacity curtailed city gates during transitions and where the city gate is only partly open. Prices do not stay within the narrow limits that one finds between the fields and market centers. It is not distance alone that makes the difference, for very distant market centers are highly integrated with production fields and their prices track one another closely. It is access through the city gate that matters and the gate is not open far enough yet. City gates also lack the sorts of market institutions that serve the interstate market so well.

NOTES

1. More recently, the California Public Utility Commission mandated that major gas distribution utilities become open access carriers for their industrial (non-core) customers. Furthermore, the gas distributors must allocate a portion of their transmission rights on the long-haul pipelines to the non-core customers. See California Public Utility Commission, Order Instituting Rulemaking into Natural Gas Procurement and Reliability Issues, Decision No. 91-11-025, November 6, 1991.

2. See *Inside FERC*, "California core market customers soon can obtain transportation." March 4, 1991, p. 16.

3. There are $N(NL + 1)$ possible arbitrage paths, and $N = 3$ and $L = 3$.

4. In order to deliver gas at the same price, they must discount their tariffs to interruptible shippers. Market-driven interruptible tariffs are a desirable side benefit of the competition that open access has brought to gas markets.

5. The number of arbitrage paths of length $\leq D$ expands at a power D of the links in the system.

6. Cointegration techniques were discussed in the previous chapter.

7. See Engle and Granger (1987).

8. The discussion of the empirical results follows Walls (1994c).

9. Four lags were used in the unit root tests on the residuals from the cointegrating regressions. This lag length assured that the residuals from the testing equation were white noise. The results of the cointegration tests were

not sensitive to the number of lags included in the testing equation.

10. See Lütkepohl (1991, pp. 43–59) for a discussion of impulse response analysis in multivariate time series models.

11. To account for the historical (contemporaneous) correlation in the residuals, we use the Choleski factorization, which is the standard method.

12. It is not, strictly speaking, appropriate to make inference from the impulse response functions without confidence limits (Cooley and LeRoy, 1985). Walls (1992) computed confidence bands using a parametric bootstrap suggested by Kloek and Van Dijk (1978). The results showed that the confidence bands were tight relative to the magnitude of the price changes.

Chapter 7

Gas Prices and the Futures Market

Most gas purchases are spot transactions. Because prices are volatile, a futures market can promote greater efficiency by allowing gas users and suppliers to hedge against the risk of future price changes. If they can hedge effectively, they will be less adverse to undertaking projects that are worthwhile, but risky. A futures contract permits sellers and buyers to lock in future prices, even though their deals are made in a volatile spot market. If they can hedge price risk effectively through futures contracts, they will be less reluctant to rely on the spot market. Moreover, an organized futures market is a mechanism for discovering price where trades are documented and the delivery mechanism is well known. Here, less informed traders can get estimates of prices where trades are made in a competitive atmosphere and price information is broadly available. Small traders can acquire future supplies in a competitive market as well. For all these reasons, a futures market can promote a better spot market. Has the futures market done this? That is the question we address in this chapter.

WHAT A FUTURES MARKET DOES

There are two properties that one looks for in a futures market: Does the futures price move with the spot price so that hedging is effective? How well does the futures price forecast the future price that will hold in the spot market? We examine these two questions here. As always in this book, our focus is on pricing in the network. In this chapter, that translates into a concern for how the futures contract delivery mechanism and pricing are affected by the connection structure of the network. Is the network sufficiently open so that spot prices at every spot market on the network can be hedged against the futures price at the delivery point of the contract?

What effective hedging through the futures contract would require is that the spot price in every market on the network be connected with the futures price at the contract delivery point. It would further require that spot prices at each location be arbitraged over all of the markets. We have seen that, even though the regional gas markets have become integrated, there still remain a few points where prices are not fully arbitraged. At these points we would not expect the futures market to be a fully effective hedging mechanism. Gas distributors, utilities, and gas producers must be able to hedge against price changes at the market locations where they can purchase and deliver the commodity. So, when we look at the effectiveness of the futures market, we have to ask where it is effective and where it is not and see if its effectiveness is related to where the spot market is located and how well it is connected to other markets. We will do that by examining the relation between spot and futures prices over many spot markets, encompassing the production areas, the interconnection hubs, and the city gates.

WHAT A FUTURES MARKET REQUIRES

The major benefit of a futures market is that it allows market participants to hedge the risk of price changes that can affect their inventories, or their future purchases and sales. The success and survival of a futures market depends on how well it serves the hedging needs of gas producers, transporters, and users. An efficient and well-functioning futures market can make inventories less risky, and such inventories can smooth out seasonal or other variations in spot prices and ease the price risk that gas consumers face. Futures prices can also supply information about what level spot prices might go to in the future. Finally, in a network of markets, gas futures contracts can actually be used to arbitrage prices in two locations that are not directly connected (this was shown in Chapter 4).

Commodities to be traded in a futures market have to fulfill several requirements for the market to be successful. The commodity must be homogeneous and fungible. Gas delivered under one contract must be as good as gas delivered under another contract. It must be possible to sell the delivered commodity readily without having to take a large discount. Another way to say this is that the cash spot gas market must be characterized by a high degree of liquidity, which requires broad participation by gas buyers and sellers.

Gas must be deliverable to make the futures enforceable; if it cannot be delivered, a buyer for whom price has gone the wrong way cannot be made to buy it. The gas futures market could not begin until enough pipelines were open and connected to the network to open a path from the futures delivery point to most other points in the network. Consequently, the pipeline grid and the markets scattered over it must be open and interconnected so that gas can move over all its links, assuring that the gas resources available to the market are pooled over all sources of supply. This scenario assures the elastic supply and wide participation needed to make the cash market liquid. The more open and connected are the pipelines in the grid, the more liquid will be the underlying cash market on which the futures market is based. In addition, there must be enough price volatility in the cash market to justify hedging.

As we have seen in preceding chapters, these conditions are largely met in the open access network created by pipeline deregulation. There is an open and interconnected pipeline grid and there are many spot markets that enjoy wide participation because of their locations at interconnection points. Price volatility in the gas spot markets is assured because many factors affect the supply and demand at each market: capacity bottlenecks to large flows, volatile pipeline tariffs, shortages of interruptible transportation, changing weather, local business conditions, pumping station failures, well freeze-offs, and so on. These factors guarantee that demand and supply at every location will be subject to random changes. It is possible either directly or through other means to transfer gas among most of the markets in the network.

If the futures market is to improve the allocation of gas, the futures price must be an accurate signal of the future spot price. The effectiveness of the futures contract as a hedging instrument depends on how well the futures price forecasts the future spot price. A futures contract is a more effective hedging device when it reduces the variance of the hedger's total position (cash and futures combined), and it will do that best when the variation in the futures price explains all or most of the variation in the spot price. For this reason, a futures market is effective when the futures price is an unbiased predictor of the future spot price.

HEDGING IN A NETWORK

To be effective, the futures market must provide a way to hedge risk where buyers and sellers do business. A local distribution company that holds inventory in a city or an industrial user that buys gas at a city gate must hedge price risk there, at that place. The effectiveness with which price risk can be hedged at a city depends on how well the futures contract, which is for delivery to a different place, predicts spot prices in that city. For the futures price of gas to be delivered at the Henry Hub to predict the price of gas in, say, Chicago or Los Angeles, the market where the price is made must be arbitraged against prices in the fields. However, we have seen that some city gates are still not fully integrated into the production areas. In these markets, the effectiveness of hedging is not as great as in markets that are highly integrated with the production areas.

Capacity limits and the availability of interruptible transportation also differ throughout the network and will affect the linkage of the spot markets to the futures market. Because of these and other idiosyncratic factors, some spot markets will be more closely tied to the futures market than others. For this reason, we carry out our analysis of spot and futures prices at different points in the network to examine the effectiveness of hedging at these locations and to reach some conclusion about the overall effectiveness of hedging.

THE FUTURES CONTRACT

In April 1990, trading in a natural gas futures contract opened on the New York Mercantile Exchange.[1] A market for natural gas futures had been proposed to the FERC in 1984 but was not approved. A proposal designating a different delivery point was later approved by the FERC and then by the Chicago Futures Trading Commission (CFTC) in 1990.

Each futures contract calls for the delivery of 10,000 million Btu of natural gas, plus or minus 2 percent. This amount of energy is equivalent to 600 barrels of No. 2 heating oil. Prices are quoted in dollars and cents per million Btu, with a minimum price increment of one mill per million Btu; this amounts to a minimum tick of $10 per contract. The maximum daily price fluctuation allowed is ten cents per million Btu, or $1,000 per contract. However, there is no price fluctuation limit for the contract that is nearest its maturity date. Positions taken by traders who are not hedging a commercial transaction are limited to 350 contracts in the "spot month" and 5,000 contracts in any individual month and in all months combined. Spot month goes into effect ten business days prior to the last day of trading.

THE DELIVERY MECHANISM

In 1987, four pipelines applied to the Federal Energy Regulatory Commission to establish a delivery service at Katy, Texas, to be used for spot and futures market transactions. Katy was a natural choice for a pipeline hub due to its high degree of connectivity with intrastate and interstate gas pipelines, and its proximity to consumption and production areas. The FERC declined the application in 1989 as unnecessary due to the increasing availability of open access transportation. The New York Mercantile Exchange changed the proposed delivery point to the Sabine Pipe Line Company's Henry Hub located in Erath, Louisiana. The Henry Hub is a pipeline interchange near production and consumption areas. It began operating in May 1988 and connects seven interstate pipelines, two intrastate pipelines, and one gathering system.

All transportation at the Henry Hub is interruptible. The probability of an interruption is especially high during periods of peak demand. Access to transportation is on a first-come first-served basis and the queue discipline is non-preemptive, that is, pipeline customers currently shipping gas cannot be preempted by another shipper with higher priority who requests service after gas has begun flowing for shippers with lower priority. Deliverability, a key condition for the success of the contract, is assured only so long as interruptible transportation is available. However, alternative delivery provisions and exchange for physicals are allowed. There can be limits to deliverability at peak times, which can limit the effectiveness of the futures market. As the market matures, however, the number of contracts where delivery is made declines to a very small percentage of the contracts made, and the interruptible constraint becomes less binding.

FUTURES AND SPOT PRICES IN A NETWORK

Every hedge is a contract for a transaction that is opposite to the trade a person intends to make. If you intend to sell gas at some future date, then you hedge against a price decline by selling a futures contract at that date. If the price of gas falls, the loss on the sale of the commodity is offset by the gain on the futures contract. The seller locks in his price by selling futures contracts appropriate to his delivery intentions in the future. The transactions will offset one another and offer a more effective hedge if the futures and spot price movements match one other. The less these prices move together, the less effectively will the futures contracts hedge spot price risk.

The extent to which futures and spot prices move so as to offer effective hedging can be put simply and directly. The futures price must converge to the spot price at maturity.[2] Furthermore, the futures price must be a fair gamble given all the information that is available. A common test for futures market efficiency is to regress the spot market price at time t on the futures contract price at time $t - j$ for a contract maturing at time t:

$$S_t = \beta_0 + \beta_{1\,t-j}F_t + \mu_t. \tag{7.1}$$

This states that the futures price at time $t - j$ estimates the spot price that will hold at time t. It should be an unbiased predictor of the future spot price and converge to it at maturity. To test how well the futures market predicts and converges to the spot market, we test the restriction that $\beta_1 = 1$. β_0 is not restricted because prices can differ by a constant, which will be related to their distance apart through transmission tariffs. Because the spot and futures markets are at different locations, their prices will not necessarily be equal, owing to transportation costs.

THE EVIDENCE

The data are a sample of 44 observations taken from June 1990 to January 1994. Futures prices are from the New York Mercantile Exchange and spot prices are from *Gas Daily*. We take the futures price to be the price at the close of trading thirty days before the last day of trading in that contract. For our first exercise, we take the closing price on the last day of trading for each futures contract spot price in the cash market.[3] The test gets at the matter of how well the futures price at any time before maturity predicts the futures price on the closing day of the contract. This gets at the idea that the futures contract must be a fair gamble and, therefore, the best estimate of the futures price at any point in the future, including at contract maturity, should be the futures price now.

For our spot market prices, we take spot prices at twelve different markets in the network. One spot market is located at the Henry Hub, the delivery point of the futures contract. The remaining spot markets are located at eight major pipeline interconnection hubs and at three city gates. Table 7.1 lists the markets by region and by pipeline.

RESULTS

Each price series was first tested for non-stationarity by looking for the presence of a unit root. We found that all the series are non-stationary. However, their first differences are stationary. This is compelling evidence that all the prices are integrated of order one and cointegration is the appropriate statistical technique to model these data.[4]

The results of the cointegration analysis are given in Table 7.1. The hypothesis that there are no cointegrating vectors $(r = 0)$ was rejected for all the spot markets, with the exception of the El Paso pipeline in the San Juan gas basin of New Mexico. In addition, we find evidence that there is only one cointegration relation between the futures market and each spot market, that is, we cannot reject the hypothesis that there is one or less cointegration relations $(r \leq 1)$. This is evidence that there is a long-run relationship preventing the spot and futures prices from diverging beyond an arbitrage limit. Of the twelve spot markets located at points other than the Henry Hub, eleven are cointegrated with the futures market. Only the one in San Juan Basin is not. Beyond being cointegrated, we want to see if the futures price at Henry Hub is an unbiased forecaster of the spot price at the twelve other regional markets. Operationally the unbiasedness is quantified by testing the hypothesis that the cointegrating parameter β_1 is equal to unity. It is for all the markets but Transco pipeline in East Texas, Panhandle pipeline in Oklahoma, and Northwest pipeline in the Rockies.[5]

Table 7.1
Cointegration Analysis on Spot and Futures Prices
June 1990–January 1994

Location/Pipeline Node	$H : r = 0$	$H_0 : r \leq 1$	$\hat{\beta}_0$	$\hat{\beta}_1$	$H : \beta_1 = 1$
Cash Spot Price	21.476^a	7.123	0.075	0.841	1.29
Henry Hub Spot Price	20.083^a	6.214	0.145	0.738	2.58
West Texas—El Paso	22.129^a	7.844	-0.143	1.130	0.41
East Texas—Transco	20.029^a	5.890	-0.296	1.460	5.29^a
North Texas—NGPL	20.507^a	6.344	-0.316	1.420	3.56
South Texas—Trunkline	21.050^a	6.967	-0.243	1.350	3.48
Louisiana—ANR	20.242^a	6.588	-0.226	1.357	3.79
Oklahoma—Panhandle	20.399^a	5.383	-0.311	1.406	3.93^a
San Juan Basin—El Paso	19.029	4.275	—	—	—
Rockies—Northwest	20.663^a	2.011	-0.569	1.646	8.10^a
Midwest City Gate	22.126^a	6.543	-0.113	1.270	2.93
California City Gate	24.058^a	8.654	-0.095	1.131	2.72
Chicago City Gate	22.285^a	5.477	-0.094	1.304	3.45

[a]Denotes that the null hypothesis was rejected at the 5 percent marginal significance level. The 5 percent critical values for the cointegration rank tests are from table 1* of Osterwald-Lenum (1992): For $H_0 : r = 0$ the critical value is 19.96 and for $H_0 : r \leq 1$ the critical value is 9.24. The 5 percent critical value for the hypothesis that $\beta_1 = 1$ is 3.84.

Source: Walls (1995).

Figure 7.1
Spot Price (S_t) and Futures Price ($_{t-1}F_t$)

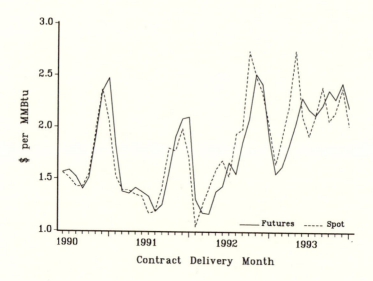

Source: Walls (1995).

Of particular interest is that the data do not reject market efficiency at the city-gate markets. Prices in the futures market accurately reflect the future spot price of natural gas at these locations up to the cost of transmission. Commitments made at these locations can be hedged effectively in the futures market.

Finally, the futures price at any month before closing of the contract accurately forecasts the closing futures price (first row of the table). In the Henry Hub spot market, the futures price is an unbiased predictor of the future spot price (second row of the table). The spot and futures prices plotted in Figure 7.1 show clearly how well they track one another.

CONCLUSIONS

Much of the pipeline network is sufficiently open to assure the deliverability required to support exchange in the futures market. The futures contract supplies an effective hedging mechanism for participants in those spot markets where spot and futures price move together. This is the case in most of the markets we analyzed, though there are many other markets for which this determination remains to be made. We have no knowledge as to why the San Juan Basin and Rocky Mountain areas show price behavior that makes the futures contract a less satisfactory device for hedging there than at other locations. Both are supply basins that are somewhat more susceptible to well freeze-offs than many of the other supply basins. Beyond that guess, we have no conjectures.

The good news is that the futures market is alive and well and its price discovery mechanism is reliable and unbiased. The futures market price is an unbiased predictor of the future spot price at its point of delivery, and it is an unbiased predictor, up to transmission cost differences, of spot prices at most other markets. The contract offers gas suppliers, users, and traders an effective hedge against price risk and a good estimate of where gas prices are headed.

NOTES

1. The description of the natural gas futures contract is drawn largely from Dearborn (1990).

2. There is evidence that in the early trading periods the spot and futures prices did not converge reliably (Walls, 1993). However, the delivery mechanism has been refined so that spot and futures prices now converge as predicted by the theory.

3. Because there must be no unexploited arbitrage opportunities at contract expiration, it must be the case that $S_t =_t F_t$.

4. See Walls (1995) for the details of the statistical testing.

5. Market efficiency was tested by imposing the restriction that $\beta_1 = 1$. The constant term is not restricted to zero to allow for transportation costs.

Part III

Competitive Institutions for Networks

Chapter 8

Assessing Competitiveness

In this chapter we try to draw some conclusions from our survey of open access and the evolution of markets. We are keenly interested in taking stock of what our findings as to the structure and functional performance of natural gas markets teach us about how to measure monopoly and competition. Open access has given us a glimpse of what market competition really looks like in natural gas, the first such view that can actually inform us as to how markets would work in this industry. What we have seen is very different from what the theory of regulated monopoly says should have happened. According to this theory, competition is unsuited to natural gas; it would lead to wasteful duplication, would not efficiently coordinate the use of the pipeline network, and would produce erratic price behavior. The evidence we have assembled speaks to the operation of competitive markets with clarity and unanimity: competition made gas prices converge over the network, eliminating pockets of non-responsive and possibly monopolistic prices, and integrated markets. The gas market is functionally competitive.

What does functional competitiveness imply about the validity of the structural measures of monopoly and competition of the kind the Federal Energy Regulatory Commission applies to regional markets? It will be clear by now that we regard the interconnections and paths in the pipeline network as the fundamental structural elements in the determination of prices. Open access and flexible transmission create the functional paths on this structure and they are assembled in response to prices and arbitrage opportunities. The market is functionally competitive if it produces competitive prices, whatever its structure. The gas market is competitive if the spatial distribution of prices over the network exhibits the right kind of convergence and dynamics. We address this issue more fully in this chapter.

Our point is simple: competition is as competition does and this is to be inferred from the price evidence. Price evidence is functional and far more compelling than structural evidence. Moreover, our results indicate that structure and prices are essentially unrelated in today's gas market. Among the questions we address are the following: How would the competitive conditions in a market be evaluated using the methods we develop in this book? Why did markets work so well? What is it about the way they were organized that made them do so well what the standard theory of regulation says they cannot do? We close by briefly applying these lessons to electricity and other network industries.

MEASURING MONOPOLY AND COMPETITION

The emergence of markets poses problems for the Federal Energy Regulatory Commission; by what method can it determine the existence of competition and the potential for anticompetitive action by companies they regulate? The 1992 Energy Policy Act makes competition a standard by which to judge the public interest. The commission's determination of when "market-based pricing" is acceptable policy centers around how they ascertain the competitiveness of a market. This question is paramount in cases involving gas pipeline restructuring under Order 636.

The Federal Energy Regulatory Commission relies on antitrust methods to judge competitiveness. This method is wrong in today's gas market and it must change. The method relies entirely on structural elements of the market to determine competitiveness.[1] The method defines the "relevant antitrust market" by asking how many suppliers within a geographic area would have to collude to raise prices by some arbitrary percentage. This calculation incorporates substitution among competing products in the same geographic area and from the supply available to the market from other areas. The availability of supplies from other areas is taken to be a matter of how many pipelines connect these areas with the market in question. If all the gas comes over just one line, then that pipeline has a share equal to the entire market and is judged, by this method, to have monopoly power. If there are two lines, then their capacity to flow gas into the area becomes a factor in the calculation, and so on for three or more pipelines.

There may be allowances for how easy it is to connect to a nearby, presently unconnected, pipeline and other such factors. Nevertheless the whole exercise is based on structure, not on how prices in that market are made and how they relate to prices in other markets at other locations. After all, the Federal Energy Regulatory Commission is worried about prices, so why not go to prices for evidence of competitiveness? Looking at Herfindahl-Hirschman indices and other structural measures is inferior to looking at prices, which are the final matter of concern. With our methods, the computations are easier for they do not rely on judgments about geographic areas, the likelihood of collusion, or who might enter under what circumstances. To use our methods, one estimates the vector autoregression and cointegration models using price data and looks for rejections of the network law of one price. This is what we have done and we will put the method to work here to show how a competitiveness determination can be made using our models of arbitrage, cointegration, price dynamics, and correlation.[2]

The Network Law of One Price and Competitiveness

If a market is competitive, its price cannot be out of line with prices in other markets. Competition involves the ability to sell and buy over many markets and its hallmark is that it is not possible to arbitrage prices for a sure gain. That is, if market i is competitive, then its price should be within the cost of arbitrage of prices in all other markets.

We tested the network law of one price in the fields, hubs, and city gates by estimating the equation system

$$\Delta p_{1,t} = \omega_1 W_t + \gamma_{1,1,0} + \sum_{l=1}^{L} \sum_{j=1}^{N} \gamma_{1,j,l} \Delta p_{j,t-l} + \epsilon_{1,t}$$

$$\vdots$$

$$\Delta p_{i,t} = \omega_2 W_t + \gamma_{2,2,0} + \sum_{l=1}^{L} \sum_{j=1}^{N} \gamma_{i,j,l} \Delta p_{j,t-l} + \epsilon_{i,t} \qquad (8.1)$$

$$\vdots$$

$$\Delta p_{N,t} = \omega_N W_t + \gamma_{N,N,0} + \sum_{l=1}^{L} \sum_{j=1}^{N} \gamma_{N,j,l} \Delta p_{j,t-l} + \epsilon_{N,t}$$

and checking for the condition that $\gamma_{i,j,l} = 0$ between all market-pairs i, j in the network of N markets and for all time lags $l = 1 \ldots 3$. We found that the price at each market incorporates the information contained in past prices at all the other markets. If the network law of one price holds over a group of spatially separated markets, then they are all within arbitrage limits of one another and, therefore, they are in the same market. If a market's price behavior says it is in the same market with all the rest, this is the overriding factor, whether or not it is served by one or many pipelines. If a market is capacity constrained or if its prices are monopolistically determined, then some of the parameters of $\gamma_{i,j,l}$ will not equal zero.

What we found is that the condition $\gamma_{i,j,l} = 0$ held for all the fields in our sample, all hubs but one, and for several, but not all, city gates. All the markets that pass the arbitrage test would have to be taken to be competitive; those that did not bear closer examination.

Cointegration and Competitiveness

Now consider two series of prices, p_i and p_j and their linear transformation:

$$p_{j,t} - \alpha - \beta p_{i,t} = \mu_t \qquad (8.2)$$

Market integration requires that the estimated parameter $\hat{\beta}$ in the cointegrating regression be equal to one.

Our cointegration analysis compared pairs of markets and found that about three-quarters of the combined field and hub markets are cointegrated (see Table 5.2 in Chapter 5 for a report on these results). All of these market-pairs would pass the competitiveness test.

The market integration statistic for nearly all market-pairs drifts upward over the entire sample period and this can be interpreted to indicate that most pairs became more strongly cointegrated. By the end of the sample in 1991, the degree of cointegration between distant market-pairs approached the cointegration of near pairs. Thus, these markets have become more competitive over time.

An important finding is that the level of cointegration of a market was not found to depend on the number of pipelines in the market area. This casts doubt on the usefulness of structural measures of competitiveness used by the Federal Energy Regulatory Commission such as pipeline counts or the Herfindahl-Hirschman index. These measures shed no light on price behavior in the relevant market. The cointegrated markets are functionally competitive and this performance is unrelated to their structural measure of competitiveness.

In many respects, our most powerful evidence came from the analysis of the futures market in Chapter 7. The futures market is unarguably competitive. One can use the futures market as a source of supply as well as to arbitrage a market price against others. Hence, any price that is cointegrated with the futures market must also be competitive. A sure test of competitiveness is a good match between a market price and the competitive futures price. This test is perhaps the simplest one to apply of all the tests proposed here. What we found in our analysis is that there is a high degree of cointegration of most field and hub prices with the futures market. An anomaly for the point of view of this test is the San Juan Basin.

Price Dynamics and Competitiveness

A competitive market has good price dynamics. If market i is linked competitively to the network of markets, then it can draw supplies from the pooled resources of all those markets. Price shocks at any market should be strongly damped by supply responses over the network. Our analysis of price dynamics made use of the estimates of the γ matrix of the vector autoregression model to examine several markets. This analysis shows how the entire network responds to a shock somewhere in the system and how long it takes. It tells us where convergence is strong and where it is not, strong convergence being associated with competitiveness.

An example of the kind of convergence experiment one can do with the model is shown in Figure 8.1, which is taken from Chapter 5. This network included the following pipelines and market areas: El Paso in West Texas, Trunkline in East Texas, Panhandle in North Texas, NGPL in South Texas, Tennessee in Louisiana, and Northern in Oklahoma. The price response in this network in 1989–1990 shows that price shocks are absorbed over all the markets in the network within a day or two. This is pretty convincing evidence that they are competitive with one another and work together to reduce price variation. This evidence also indicates that the San Juan Basin anomaly we found in our other analysis is related to the westward movement of gas through the Los Angeles city gate and not to its links to the North and East.

Spatial Correlation Patterns

The final method for determining competitiveness that we develop makes the spatial pattern of prices more apparent than our other results. We can look at the markets in which price correlation exceeds a critical value. If the correlation of the price in a market exceeds, say, 0.99 with k other markets, then that market could be said to be in a market of dimension $k + 1$. The correlation dimension of point i then is the number of row i elements of the correlation matrix that exceed a critical level. Table 8.1 gives the correlation dimension of twenty-two markets.

We have chosen a very high, 0.99, correlation value for the calculations in this table. We cover most of the major southwestern supply basins and many major pipelines. It is apparent that open access and the gas market matured from 1988 to 1990; the number of markets with which each market in the first column is highly correlated grows over time for most markets. Just a few do not show growth in their correlation dimension.[3] The West Texas market area shows the same unusual behavior we found in our previous analyses of the futures market and the Los Angeles city gate. Taken together, this evidence suggests that there is a capacity limit from West Texas through the Los Angeles city gate. It may be on the pipelines supplying gas from West Texas or on the distribution system behind the city gate; wherever it is, gas is not getting through at a pace that would tightly link the Los Angeles city gate and the West Texas supply basins with the rest of the gas market.

Figure 8.1
Price Propagation across Network 1, 1989–1990
Price Responses on the El Paso Pipeline in West Texas

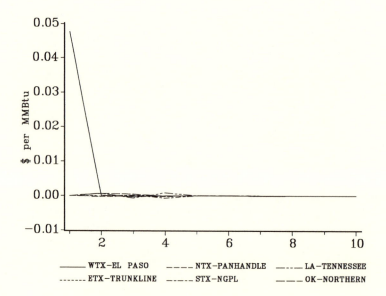

Table 8.1
Correlation Dimension of Selected Gas Markets

Point	1988 Dimension	1990 Dimension
WTX-El Paso	2	2
WTX-TRANSW	2	2
ETX-NGPL	12	16
ETX-TENN	10	15
ETX-TRUNK	8	18
NTX-ANR	3	17
NTX-NGPL	7	11
NTX-NORTH	3	4
NTX-PEPL	3	17
STX-NGPL	3	12
STX-TENN	7	15
LA-ANR	8	13
LA-COLUMB	8	11
LA-NGPL	6	12
LA-SONAT	1	9
LA-TENN	5	9
LA-TEXGAS	4	3
LA-TRUNK	3	9
LA-UNITED	0	8
OK-ANR	3	5
OK-NGPL	3	5
OK-NORTH	2	4

Summing up Competitiveness

Structural measures of competitiveness do not reflect function. They are out of date given the structural changes that have taken place in the gas industry. Not only is interruptible transportation traded in an open and competitive market; firm transportation is now in the hands of some fifteen hundred or more shippers. If the distribution companies that hold most of the rights to firm transportation can use these rights to carry gas to every city gate on the line, then the monopoly supply chain is broken, and every market becomes contestable.

The ability to trade for interruptible transmission and the availability of post-Order 636 capacity trading will remove entry barriers to sellers in every market, no matter how many pipelines serve them. No pipeline will have power over entry of transport customers. Transmission trading, in conjunction with the well-organized spot markets, will make every point on the network contestable. Even with only interruptible transmission and less than complete open access at the city gates, prices have already converged to an arbitrage-free equilibrium over most markets on the pipeline network.

Structural or Functional Analysis

We must drop a structural measure of competition in favor of a functional one. There are several reasons for this. First, it is function that matters. Any structural organization of the gas market that can deliver competitive prices is functionally competitive, no matter how it is structured. Second, it is time to drop the false ideal of perfect competition. This model itself is wholly structural in content and not a model of function. The conditions that the model assumes are neither necessary nor sufficient for competitive pricing. Our results show that very clearly, since virtually none of these conditions are met and yet the gas market is functionally competitive, based on the price evidence.

The third and most telling point is that what is called perfect competition, and held up to be the ideal that regulation should strive to emulate, is a very poor market structure. It is maladaptive to changing circumstances. It does not deliver products with the kind of variety that is required to serve the diverse customers who populate the gas business. It is non-innovating; in fact, it just assumes that there is a product that customers want without ever telling how it is discovered. It does not capture the noise and chaos which any adaptive market must possess and which any real market exhibits.

Far from perfection, perfectly competitive markets do not function well because they share certain characteristics with planning. In planning, all the equations of the system are solved by the planning bureau who then calls out allocations or prices to managers whose Lange-Lerner behavioral rules tell them to set marginal cost equal to price. The model of perfect competition is similar in that in it markets solve the problem of computing a price vector, and profit-maximizing managers do the rest. Neither task is doable and the solutions they would obtain, if they could find them, are inept and narrow.

Competition is more like evolution than it is like solving a well-defined system of equations. Evolution is robust and opportunistic; it searches a broad landscape and promotes diversity. Selection eliminates the weak solutions and noise presents new alternatives for selection to affect. This is precisely what we have seen in the gas market as it has evolved over the past decade of relaxed regulation.

It is time to stop apologizing for competition on the grounds that it is not perfect; perfect competition, like any homogeneous and noiseless process, is incapable of evolving and its structural perfection is its greatest weakness. It is a great irony that the model of perfect competition has become a strong source of intellectual support for regulation and antitrust on the grounds that most markets are imperfectly competitive. There is less irony to the point when one recognizes that the planning model and the perfectly competitive model are the same. There is less irony still in the point when one recognizes that it is easier to build a case for regulation if markets are held up to an unattainable ideal.

Not only is the perfectly competitive ideal unattainable, it is irrelevant and undesirable. It is irrelevant because it is a structural and not a functional ideal. It is undesirable because markets with perfectly competitive structure work very badly. The reason perfectly competitive markets do not exist is because they can not stand up to the evolutionary pressure from their messy and imperfectly competitive market competitors.

DISSOLVING MONOPOLY

We argued in Chapter 2 that a system in which the ownership of transmission capacity is decentralized is apt to be competitive. This is so because transmission will be allocated by many agents who do not consider how their trades affect the prices received by the other owners. The interruptible transmission market approaches this decentralized form of trading, and it has been an effective instrument for dissolving monopoly. Interruptible trading is competitive and it is a substitute for firm transmission. Hence, competitive discipline is imposed on firm prices by the interruptible market.

An even stronger discipline on firm transmission pricing is gas pricing. Gas delivered into a market must be competitive with all the other sources of supply that are capable of delivering into that market. This includes almost every other market on the network for two reasons: gas is deliverable everywhere in the network if there are open access, offsets, and futures trading, and other means can be used to arbitrage an out-of-line gas price even when there is no direct connection. Hence, firm transmission must be priced so that whoever uses it can deliver gas into the market at prices that will meet the competition from all other sources. A reading of our price evidence then forces the conclusion that there already are strong forces in the gas market to discipline firm transmission rates.

Capacity Trading

More liberalized capacity trading would give pipeline users the ability to vertically connect segments on lines by acquiring the appropriate capacity rights. Horizontally integrated pipeline networks can be created through the acquisition of transmission rights on connecting lines. These new pipeline structures would, in effect, constitute a form of new entry into the pipeline business. These entrants would have a more web-like structure than the linear pipelines that have dominated the industry under FERC certification procedures. These web structures would integrate larger segments of the pipeline grid and would be capable of putting together deals and transactions that linear pipelines cannot do. They could compete in many markets simultaneously and would be a powerful competitive force. They have no potential for monopolization because they own or use only portions of each of the pipelines on which they organize their web structure.

Capacity Release

Pipeline structure under the rules of capacity release and trading does decentralize the allocation of capacity, but it does not go far enough or offer enough flexibility. The transfer of pipeline transmission capacity to the holders of gas purchase contracts has decentralized the allocation of transportation capacity—as many as sixty or seventy agents may hold the capacity on a given pipeline.[4] Yet, open access is incomplete. The local distribution companies that acquired firm transportation are not allowed to sell it. Their incentives to release it for short-term use are distorted by the rate making of Rule 636. That is, unused transportation capacity reverts to the pipeline and not the holder.

Transportation is restricted under Rule 636 in several ways: transmission capacity rights cannot directly be transferred to others; they cannot be subdivided or combined on a line; nor can segments over separate pipelines be joined; there is limited flexibility in changing injection and withdrawal points; restrictions on transmission tariffs still apply. These restrictions limit flexibility and prevent the use of decentralized methods for allocating transportation capacity; they are the remaining barrier to a more competitive market in transportation. They safely can be removed, given what the price evidence indicates.

Contracting around Monopoly

As we argued in Chapter 2, contracting is a way to circumvent monopoly. Increasing the variety of contracts expands the number of ways that a monopoly can be contested. Under open access, the scope and variety of contracts have expanded. Lyon and Hackett (1993) describe the contracts that have emerged because of the opportunities afforded by open access. They also call attention to the limitations on contracts and governance structures that are mandated by the Open Access Orders, particularly Order 636. The ability to contract outside the traditional services mandated by regulation allows gas transactions to be more closely tailored to what the customer wants and lets them do an end run around monopoly.

The existence of many parallel markets—along with the expanded scope of contracting and the freedom to organize new institutions—has given a new pluralism and adaptability to the gas market. It is possible for the industry to experiment with alternative contracts, organizational forms, and institutions in order to search out and discover new, more effective ways of doing things. Smaller and more unusual users are more readily accommodated. New solutions can be devised and tested without making wholesale, systemwide changes that are often required by regulation. The basis has, at least in part, been established for the industry to organize itself to adapt readily and efficiently to change.

WHY MARKETS WORKED

Markets succeeded because open access gave them scope to operate, let new kinds of traders into the market, and gave traders the means to trade over wide areas. Four factors account for this:

- Market transactions between gas suppliers and users replaced the pipeline merchant.

- Gas transactions are made within a competitive market institution created by the industry itself.

- Transportation trading evolved an interconnected grid of pipelines in place of the closed and balkanized grid that preceded open access.

- This open and interconnected grid supplies the means for price arbitrage.

Open access and transportation trading make it possible to create a more connected grid of pipelines with flexible routings, and this more connected pipeline grid expanded the power of arbitrage to discipline prices over all points of gas supply and use. It was instrumental in eliminating entry barriers.

Contesting Markets

Trade in interruptible transmission made it possible to enter and exit a market quickly and without making irreversible commitments. A supplier who wishes to contest a market need not construct a new pipeline to do it, and so they no longer are faced with high fixed costs of entering and exiting markets. Thus, the "hit and run" entry of contestable markets theory has been put in place in gas markets by allowing gas and interruptible transportation to be actively traded among a variety of participants.[5]

Buyers and sellers of gas in every market compete throughout the network. Suppliers can contest any market to which they can deliver gas at a competitive price, and gas can flow across the network to eliminate price disparities. Even those markets served by only one pipeline have available to them sources of supply from a wide network.

Institution Building

Markets succeeded under open access because participants built effective institutions to govern their trade in gas and transportation. Under these institutions, markets have achieved a high degree of coordination between commodity trading and transportation. The bidweek auction is one of the coordinating institutions. It is an open auction that has strong competitive properties even with few traders; this has been shown both theoretically and empirically. The wide participation and strong institutions of the bidweek auction offer assurance that, for the available supply, the price is competitively determined.

The bidweek auction coincides with the week in which shippers make their nominations to the pipelines for the amounts they intend to ship the next month. During the auction and nomination period, shippers are able to buy simultaneously the gas they intend to ship and arrange for its transportation. Those who hold firm transportation contracts have guaranteed transportation up to the limit of their contract. They are able to buy the spot commodity with the assurance that they can ship any quantity up to their transmission limit.

Brokers who buy the commodity to ship via interruptible transportation can make and unmake deals on the commodity throughout bidweek as they observe the amount of firm transportation nominated by those who hold it. They have real-time information on the amount of capacity booked, which they use to make their commodity commitments.

These institutions support a wide range of trading of transportation and natural gas over the vast network of pipelines that connect markets with supply basins. These wide trading networks give the market depth and liquidity, and they have unleashed the force of arbitrage to discipline prices.

Arbitrageurs

Brokers are middlemen who buy and sell wherever they can. They are not committed to a particular buyer, seller, or location; they will buy and sell wherever the prices make a trade profitable. They search for opportunities and they help their clients find better terms. Arbitrageurs make price differences disappear whenever they are large enough to grant a profit.

Countless numbers of brokers buy and sell gas throughout the pipeline network, even though they do not have uninterruptible transmission rights of their own. They aggregate supplies from producers and demands from users. By purchasing interruptible transmission from various pipelines, they can ship gas over flexible supply networks which they fashion by combining transmission on one or more pipelines. Some brokers hold a portfolio of gas demand and supply contracts, which they match continuously. Others act as the purchasing agent for downstream local distribution companies. Brokers also deal with customers who are behind the city gate; they can get through the city gate and give their customers access to the best interstate deals when the distribution company permits them to bypass its merchant function.

ELECTRICITY AND OTHER NETWORK MARKETS

There are a host of industries to which these findings might apply. Many industries are configured as networks; air transport is a network of routes. Likewise the shipping and trucking industries are organized as route networks. Telecommunications and electricity are nearer to natural gas in their network form, and it is these that we consider in light of our work on the competitiveness of markets with network structure.

In order to use prices as evidence of competitiveness, of course, one must have price data from markets. The electricity industry does have very active markets that make prices at locations all over the power grid.

Transmission

New transmission technology and control systems broadened the opportunities for markets during the 1960s and 1970s. The bulk power market evolved in step with this technology; in this market, utilities made long-term agreements to trade power with one another. It was soon followed by a spot power market for so-called economy energy.

Utilities developed pooling agreements to share generation resources over regional networks. The agreements expanded the territories over which electricity was transmitted and wheeling power through the grid began. With wheeling came the question of access.

Access

Like customers located behind the city gate of a gas distributor, customers located inside an electrical utility's service area could not purchase power unless they could get access to wheel power through the local grid. Equally, the point applies to a power transaction that involves utilities located on opposite sides of an intervening utility's territory. To transact, they must be able to wheel the power through the intervening utility's grid.

With pooling and wheeling, the industry began to dissolve the territorial boundaries erected under the Public Utility Holding Company Act and subsequent regulation by federal and state authorities who carved territories into jurisdictional protectorates. As in the gas industry, access began to promote a more integrated power grid.

The advantages of an interconnected power grid are many. Generating resources could be pooled, load variations could be smoothed over the many markets and users on the grid, diverse customers could be combined into portfolios that balance loads by time and direction of flow, and power could flow from low-cost generators to replace high-cost generators. An active network of markets, which makes prices daily or by the hour, supplies the information needed to direct energy flows over the network of resources and users so as to minimize the total cost of electricity.

As in the gas industry, access means that buyers and sellers could deal directly. It also means that they can search over the network for the best price. This ability to search puts competitive pressure on the local utility to supply cheaper power.

Applying the Lessons from Gas

Because power pools, wheeling, and energy trading have a long history in the electricity industry, the necessary institutions and practices are in place for a smoother transition to markets than natural gas had. In the gas industry, the institutions and practices took some time to emerge and evolve to a level of refinement that let markets operate well. Our results suggest that several years were required to get smooth operation in gas markets even after open access was a completed property of the pipeline network. It seems to have taken this long to build the institutions, the interconnections, and to educate traders in the operation of markets.

A transition to markets should take less time in the electricity industry.

The interconnections are in place, institutions are well developed, and traders already have the required experience; the transition should be more rapid and sure in the electricity industry than it was in the gas industry. Even so, the transition in gas was rapid and well-organized. Yet the organization of gas markets came from the industry itself, not from on high. That should not be forgotten in the electricity industry. The FERC should stay out of the way so that markets can work out the details of the agreements and sorts of rights and contracts that are needed to make competition effective.

Complications

We understand that electricity flows over the network as Ohm's law prescribes and cannot be confined readily to a linear path. This property and emergent properties of a non-linear network flow, such as loop flow, complicate the access issue. However, gas flowing through a network under pressure follows the path of least resistance too, and in a highly interconnected grid of pipelines gas is not unlike electricity in this important sense: the delivery of gas and of electricity to points in the grid is a network flow problem. Maximum flow through the system requires that all the links be used in the right way.

Prices that are made daily or hourly or even by ten-minute intervals in spot markets scattered over the grid can supply the information needed to guide the flow of electricity through the network, producing it at the lowest cost generators and sending it to the markets where its value is highest. With prices made continuously in a network of markets, the flow of energy can take place nearly in real time. Moreover, prices reflect the state of the network at each trading interval and they can supply state information to guide flows through the network. The signal that the process is working is the convergence of prices over the network, just as we have seen in the gas industry.

Therefore, we should be looking at prices—spot, contract, and utility retail prices—over the power grid for evidence of competitiveness. Structural features like the number of lines into or out of a territory are important only if prices are out of line. Yet it is the price evidence that is decisive. Prices are unlikely to fail to track the competitive arbitrage band, as we saw in natural gas, if the power grid is open and competitive market institutions are in place.

Transmission Trading

If the power grid is open, there will be many paths between markets (recall the computation relating paths and connections in Chapter 4). This access arms the grid with the power of arbitrage to force competitive transmission pricing. The ability to deliver power to a market at prices that are competitive with other sources caps transmission prices.

Unlike gas pipelines, the concept of shared transmission capacity has been used in electricity for some time. The industry could build on this established practice to develop a tradeable transmission right or contract. It would be tied to operational constraints that are needed to make the network work properly. In many respects, the industry has already worked out many of these details in their wheeling and pooling arrangements. It is a short step from there to a tradeable transmission right. This is another area where the electricity industry is on surer ground to make a transition to markets than the natural gas industry was at the beginning of open access.

It surely is better for the industry to work out these coordinating details than for the FERC to do it. The details are critical and must be driven by location and time specific information which a regulatory body is ill equiped to determine. There will doubtless be many kinds of agreements and transmission trades because they must be adapted to a host of differing circumstances; there is no universal arrangement and this is what a commission coping with impossible complexity will try to produce or mandate. The market has taken hold and the barriers and constraints to competition will fall as customers seek its advantages.

CONCLUSIONS

The transition from planned industry to markets in natural gas was easier than one would have been led to expect. A believer in what the theory of regulation claims would not have prepared for what happened. Market participants created the institutions that were required to support competitive exchange in gas and interruptible transmission. Access to transmission opened paths in the network and let arbitrage force prices to converge to a spatial distribution that is competitive. None of the dire predictions of the theory of regulated natural monopoly about competition and markets came true. The transition to markets in other network industries could learn these lessons.

NOTES

1. Gallick's (1993) study is as reasonable and well done as a study of this kind can be. He finds little potential for the exercise of monopoly pricing in gas markets.

2. The reader is referred to Chapters 4 through 7 for our discussion of the theory and econometrics of the method as well as the detailed evidence.

3. One way to compute the increase in correlation between more distant vertices in the later time period is to compute the condition number for each correlation matrix. The condition number is the ratio of the largest character-

istic value of the matrix to the smallest. It measures the degree of collinearity of the columns in the correlation matrix with a high condition number indicating high collinearity (Belsley et al., 1980). The condition numbers for 1988, 1989, and 1990 are 7.03×10^{16}, 1.43×10^{18}, and 2.28×10^{22}, respectively. The increasing condition numbers indicate that the correlations are becoming more equal between all pairs of vertices. The condition number of the network is an indication of how strongly connected it is and how many paths there are between vertices.

4. See Bradley (1991).

5. See Baumol, Panzar, and Willig (1988).

Chapter 9

Policy

In this chapter, we look at what our results indicate about policy. How can we design a policy that will promote the evolution of an efficient and competitive industry? We have several main points to make about how to do that:

- Forget about static efficiency; no one knows where the industry is headed or how it will need to adapt to future circumstances; adopt an evolutionary view of efficiency.

- The network is not a public utility; do not treat it like one.

- Let the market make network access an asset.

- Change the regulator's incentives.

- Release the hostages—these include the industry and its customers—by making regulation voluntary.

EFFICIENCY

The theoretical case in support of the efficiency of regulated natural monopoly founders on complexity and dynamics. In the theory, efficiency is a static concept: price at marginal cost for first-best or average cost for second-best efficiency (second-best pricing ensures the firm can survive without subsidy). These pricing mechanisms assume that we know what ought to be produced and how best to do that. However, we can only learn through trial and error, with an abundant amount of feedback to drive incentives and selection for successful products and organizational forms. Where are these to come from and who has the incentives to take the risks to learn these things? The theory of regulation is silent about these highly salient issues.

What form do learning and feedback take in a regulated natural monopoly? How are they related to efficiency? No one knows. There are several notions of efficiency at issue. First, there is the kind of local efficiency of the theory of regulation that calls for productive and allocative efficiency in a situation where we have all the requisite information to do that. This is a local form of efficiency in the sense that one is doing local hill climbing on a well-defined and known portion of a complex landscape of alternatives; that kind of efficiency is strictly second order in magnitude. A global form of efficiency is related to search over the entire landscape of alternatives for the best of those we currently know. The landscape is complex and when we move from one point to another we are moving in a fog; we only know that we have reached a better point after we move there. Many moves will be to lower valued outcomes and, so, feedback and learning are essential in order to preserve gains and focus adaptation.

Regulation does strictly local optimizing (if you think it optimizes at all); adaptive and evolutionary search looks for more promising regions. Adaptive search produces innovations and these are tested against current elements in the space of products and organizations. Successful innovations are not optimal; they just work better than the options that are currently available. Nonetheless, evolutionary search is a form of adaptive hill climbing that produces and tests new candidate solutions to economic problems. When they are successful, they replace products and organizations with new, more effective ones. These innovations produce discontinuous changes in the efficiency of markets and industries. A static optimization that freezes adaptation and fixes the outcome in a local region of the space of products and organizations blocks the adaptive process that is the source of discontinuous leaps to more effective solutions.

Incorporating this view into the theory of regulation produces a very different view from the conventional one. An effective and adaptive natural gas industry demands flexible institutions. Industry design by policy makers founders on the complexity of the design problem; it is a search for local optima only. Regulatory policy that aims at a social optimum is too vague. Yet, policy that aims at a specific goal is too narrow. The attempt to optimize policy for a given goal produces a narrow optimum that lacks robustness and may be far from optimal when circumstances change.

Successful innovations in industry institutions and organizations are more likely to produce gains in efficiency than are changes in how a firm prices a particular product. These innovations are more likely to come from the interactions of the participants in the process; in other words, effective products and organizations are more likely to be self-organized rather than handed down from above.[1] We have shown that the natural gas industry has succeeded in transforming itself into a contestable industry within the scope of opportunities presented by open access.

NETWORKS ARE NOT PUBLIC UTILITIES

Public policy stands in the way of making networks work. Antitrust law, the Public Utility Company Holding Act, and a distrust of joint ventures have made it more difficult to create integrated networks. As we show in the next section, access to a network can be made into an asset that is openly and competitively exchanged. A variety of organizations can be built across the network if access become an asset. Such organizations span the network and open markets to competitive forces. Shipper ownership of gas pipelines would make shipper-pipeline incentives more compatible; such an organization is used in many network industries.

Because of regulatory and antitrust biases against such forms of network organization, networks are more apt to be segmented. The result is that the markets they serve tend to become balkanized and isolated from other parts of the network. It also means that long linear segments of pipeline, which might be owned and operated by several companies, are merged into one; this merger then forces a public utility attitude about the firm.

Compulsory access is a source of confusion and lessens the incentives to form networks. A network takes an investment and requires compatible assets and operations. If a newcomer can gain access after these investments are made, he will have gotten the fruits of these investments without paying for them. This is a disincentive to join in the first place and a limitation to forming networks.

The most important point may be that joint ownership and operations are conducive to competitive networks; this can best be supported by creating network assets, as we show next.

MAKE ACCESS AN ASSET

If fully tradeable transportation rights are permitted to exist under regulation, they almost surely will be created by the industry. With such rights, trading would mature to include firm as well as interruptible transportation. A wide and liquid market in these rights would make the industry perfectly contestable. Such a market would price gas at least as well as the present one, which is to say very efficiently. In addition, we have shown that there can be no monopoly under a system of transportation property rights. Hence, this system calls for an entirely different role for regulation.[2]

To create a market for transportation, we need to define a tradeable property right or contract. We propose the following instruments for organizing the industry: Create a property right in transportation capacity. This right would be an undiluted interest in pipeline capacity on which other users could not intrude. The holder of transportation capacity owns the right to ship volumes up to the capacity limit over the specified segment on which the right is held. Injection and withdrawal points apply to every point on the segment. The right is assignable in part or whole to others for whatever term they wish, up to the limit of the term of the right. The right can be combined or subdivided in all dimensions.

Under this system, ownership and control of transportation capacity are decentralized among many holders, and each makes its own choices as to its use or allocation.[3] As a consequence, the centralized control that is essential for the exercise of monopoly power is dissipated. A pipeline is no longer a recognizable firm; it issues a collection of capacity rights, which are broadly distributed to many owners who act independently of one another.

Since the property right is distributed among many hands, there is a need for someone to coordinate their use. The owners of pipeline capacity hire a coordinator. The coordinator runs the pipeline and its related facilities under the direction of the owners of capacity or a board they elect. The coordinator may be one of the owners of capacity or any other party the owners select. The terms paid the coordinator are set by negotiation or in a procurement auction run by the owners.

Contracting

The owners of capacity are unrestricted in their use of it. They can:

- Use it for their own shipments, in effect becoming a vertically organized segment within the pipeline.

- Contract the capacity to transport for others, in effect becoming a contract carrier on the segment they hold.

- Present themselves as common carriers.

- Devise any other service or use of their choosing, subject only to the limits of their capacity and the operating limits the owners set to coordinate their use.

The property right in capacity can be used to create contractually a variety of solutions for gas users and producers; it permits the industry to design its own organization. The form in which pipelines are presently organized can be replicated simply. The pipeline just owns and controls all of its capacity.

Any holder can elect to become a contract carrier within the limits of his or her capacity rights. Several or all holders may pool their capacities to offer contract carriage. A portfolio of contracts could be offered by each firm or each could specialize in a specific contract, creating a variety of contracts through their individual offerings. Any shipper of gas, producer, or user may own capacity. So vertically integrated firms can be implemented upstream or downstream from any point in the pipeline system. A local distribution company could own a share of transportation capacity from its territory out to its primary sources of supply. A producer could acquire transportation with which to develop new markets. Pools of small producers could integrate their production areas and achieve the high rate of deliverability of larger producers, and they could get the transportation they would need to reach industrial users or utilities they cannot now serve.

Industrial users, which now largely must rely on interruptible service, could acquire transportation to secure reliable supplies of gas. This guarantee of reliable supplies seems to be a critical step if natural gas is to become a fuel of the future and a significant alternative source of energy to users. Oil and gas do not move to industrial users via unpredictable and interruptible transportation; there is no sound reason why natural gas should.

Expanding Capacity

New rights are issued to any party that will pay for them. The existing owners can create and offer new capacity, or an independent party can propose an expansion, subject to holding existing owner's rights intact. New projects, expansions, or new links in the grid are not subject to regulatory approval. Rights on pipelines can be connected and the rights holders pay the cost of connecting capacity on separate lines. Transmission rights are issued with conventional regulatory rate-making a part of the contract. This contract passes with each exchange of rights, so that each holder is obligated to pay rates determined by a well-defined rate-making process, and the issuer (the pipeline) is entitled to receive the regulated rate for each unit of the right. The price at which transmission rights are traded is not regulated and is free to seek a market level.[4] Transmission rights are left to market determination.

Transportation rights are shares of the capacity of a pipeline and when they are sufficiently well defined they can be traded on organized exchanges. Vernon Smith and his colleagues have developed an algorithm, based in part on the clearing methods used on the Arizona Stock Exchange, that simultaneously clears gas and transportation transactions that are compatible with transmission capacities on links of the pipeline network.[5] The routing of gas flows over the network is coordinated with demands, supplies, and transportation capacity limits. The prices that are determined simultaneously clear the gas markets at each location and their transportation links. If a market using this algorithm could be implemented, it could draw wide participation and might replace the distributed markets on which we presently rely. On the other hand, there is nothing to prevent both markets from operating simultaneously, as they do now. What is essential is to permit access to be traded.

Monopoly

What will keep dispersed transportation rights from coming back under the control of the pipeline? What will happen if the rights revert to the pipeline? The network affords many paths around most bottlenecks a prospective monopolist might try to create. Since entry is not blocked, expansions or loops are readily constructed and tied into the system under the proposed institutions. This flexibility means that there is little advantage to a pipeline in attempting to gain monopoly power by purchasing its capacity. To do so would require it to buy up the bulk of capacity on a segment and reduce output while facing the risk that users will reroute their shipments or create their own capacity by tying into the open grid at strategic points. The present owners of transportation capacity will hold out for any prospective rents that might be created through this acquisition, and present users will not release their capacity to a prospective monopolist who they think will raise the price they must pay unless they receive compensation against that prospect. Networks are a powerful deterrent to monopoly. There is an open grid to which new connections may be freely added. This structure means that new segments could be created to link separated pipelines.

The Coase theorem tells us that the process for subscribing to new capacity, in the end, will not determine who eventually holds it. So we do not have to be too careful about shaping the initial allocation. Yet it is better to stack the deck against the possibility that capacity will become concentrated by dispersing ownership initially. This dispersion will protect users from a pipeline attempting to gain monopoly by purchasing capacity because they can always decline to sell their shares, and the potential profits from monopolization will be distributed to the rights holder, leaving none for the organizer.

CHANGING INCENTIVES

When the FERC controls some portion of the transportation network, it is at the cost of removing this capacity from the competitive system. Hence, there should be competition between the FERC and the competitive system for the use of this scarce capacity, which means that the FERC must bid against other users for the right to control system capacity. Such a need would only arise when the FERC perceives a need for service that the competitive system does not meet and acts to provide that service. It must raise the funds for the service from the clients it intends to serve or seek the funds from the Congress.

The "regulated" sector then is that portion of the system that the regulator, say the FERC, contracts for to supply a service for its clients. The FERC must recruit a voluntary supply of transportation capacity by offering a regulatory contract. The contract would indicate the service to be supplied and the terms.

Holders of transmission rights elect to place them in the regulated sector under the terms of the regulatory contract or to put them in the unregulated sector, including their own use. The clients of the regulator are those who choose to buy the service supplied under the regulatory contract. These buyers are not captive to the contract, but are free to seek out any service available from all suppliers, regulated or not.

Let holders of transmission rights elect to place them in the regulated sector under the contract terms that are announced by the agency. This is a real regulatory contract. Gas users can select among suppliers that agree to operate under the regulatory contract, or they can go to others. The regulatory contract could be a cost-plus contract similar in content to cost-based rate making. Unlike the present regulatory system, however, the participation of the suppliers of transportation rights must be voluntary and limited in duration by the terms of the contract.[6] If there is a supply of transportation forthcoming to the regulated sector, then it is offered to users and suppliers at the terms determined by the regulatory agency procuring the transportation.

The design of a regulatory contract will force some straight thinking about regulation. What is the product of regulation? Do we understand what the product is well enough to write clear and enforceable contracts for its delivery? Since regulatory agencies do not have budgets to buy services of the magnitude involved, will the contract be credible? Who will pay? Is the agency's commitment to restrain its actions and decisions to those contained in the contract credible? How will the regulator charge for the product it produces for users? What can the regulator contract to do that users cannot do themselves with the expanded options they have under a system of property rights in transportation capacity?

Our proposed solution to these issues is to let the regulatory agency contract for services that are not supplied by the market, when those services have a legitimate public interest and will be supported by the users or Congress. The agency should have no command and control powers, only the powers of contract and the charge to secure options and services for legitimate public interests.

FREEING HOSTAGES

Perhaps the most critical aspect of gas regulation is that it has made core users the hostages of the regulatory process.[7] Under cost-of-service rate making, core users are the residual source of funds to cover the mistakes or choices made by the other participants.[8] The obligation of the core to shoulder excess costs is the most glaring flaw of cost-based rate making. This is an obligation core users would not voluntarily take on, if they had any alternatives, and it is the first condition of the regulatory compact that ought to be reconsidered now that competition exists in the natural gas industry.

If the market leaves behind any group of disadvantaged users, the instruments are available to correct that failing. Any public or private organization or private party can contract with a core aggregator to offer a service tailored to the disadvantaged group. The design would be worked out between the customers, the provider and the supplier. If a subsidy is to be made, the provider supplies it or applies for a public grant. An alternative to contracting for the service is for the provider to acquire the gas and transportation needed to supply the targeted group. Competition between public and private suppliers will improve the offerings available to disadvantaged users.

We do not really know if there is an effective level of cross-subsidization in the present system. How we disentangle and assign the joint costs of these complex, dynamic systems is arbitrary. There are reasons to believe that costs are higher than they would be with deregulation. If this is so, then even if there is a bias toward cross-subsidization, the cross-subsidized cost to the core with regulation may still be higher than the unsubsidized cost it would bear in the absence of regulation.

Cost-based rate making does load more risk on the core than can be justified, and the attempt to cross-subsidize the core through higher rates to other users may only partly redress the burden. In order to cross-subsidize successfully, the regulator must set non-sustainable prices. To keep heavily priced users from leaving the system, their options must be cut off. Making the core captive to the process also binds the other users. This mechanism leaves most of the participants powerless and forecloses change and experimentation.

A number of state regulatory agencies have required distributors to become transporters for "non-core" end users, but some agencies have forbidden this for core end users. Core end users have expanded options when there is tradeable transportation. Core aggregation programs can be created directly through the acquisition of transportation rights. Brokers can collect customers, purchase gas on their behalf, and obtain the transportation needed to deliver. A customer group can enter the interstate market as a purchaser, with transportation guaranteed if it acquires transportation capacity by any of the many mechanisms through which it will be available.

When providers to the core are able to acquire transportation capacity and do what is needed to get good terms for the groups they represent, the focus is shifted from negotiating and testifying with the regulator to making deals privately. A public interest organization can better serve the public if it has the instruments to do so.[9] Otherwise, public interest and consumer groups are only lobbyists whose survival requires continuing regulation of the industry to provide a forum for their point of view, which may not suit the needs of the users they claim to represent. When there is a market in transportation and broad contracting, such groups must meet the market test for their services. Regulatory agencies can contract on behalf of the core and other users who may not have market clout, and their deals will be tested against those offered by aggregators and others.

LEGISLATION

We must get rid of the antitrust bias against joint ventures, and create conditions for the evolution of firms and industry organization to reshape the network adaptively to promote the efficiency of gas markets. The emphasis should be on how firms restructure themselves and the industry to capture the gains of more efficiently utilizing network resources to exploit business opportunities. This approach relies more on internal markets because fully developed external markets in transportation cannot yet develop. Here, altering firm and industry structure is the basic mechanism for organization and reorganization. Mergers and acquisitions, spinoffs, contracts for upstream and downstream service, joint operations, pooling, holding companies, or conglomerates are the combinatorics of organization and internal markets.

External reorganization of the network would operate outside the firm: a service network would be pieced together by acquiring gas contracts and interruptible transportation rights to get gas to the hubs and on through to the right points. Internal reorganization expands the scope of the firm to bring more parts of the network inside. In this case, a network would be pieced together to exploit (possibly for the longer term) arbitrage opportunities by extending new lines as part of the firm, by merging firms that form elements of the required networks, by pooling operations on common parts of a network, forming holding company-like structures, by splitting off subdivisions, and by forming new firms. They conduct business at the level where they can operate, doing the combinatorics directly with the property rights pieces or indirectly with the organizations as the pieces.

Both methods must meet capital market tests. Networks and organizations would form to pool demand and supply variations, to merge unbalanced systems, to pool across supply basins and demand points, to maximize deliverability through the network, to gain routing flexibility, to maintain adequate redundancy for reliability, to balance inventory with deliverability, to manage load variations, to go after loads (like industrial demands) that smooth load variations, to exploit local and global information through appropriate incentives and organizations, and to package organizations as ventures that are attractive to capital markets.

At some level, both these processes are interrelated and work together, though not yet, because there presently are limitations on property rights and organization structure. The FERC limits the property rights and their combinatorics; it also limits industry organization and its combinatorics. Regulation alters property rights and limits firm and industry structure. Consequently, the industry cannot self-organize to find those combinations of external and internal markets to most effectively do what is required. It cannot evolve. Evolvability is not part of the regulatory design. Its failure to exploit evolvability as an adaptive strategy may be its biggest failure. A self-organized industry almost certainly would create evolvability as one of its primary characteristics. This adaptability would give the right mix of evolutionary operators in property rights and in organization. Birth and death processes would be fundamental parts of the process.

CONCLUSIONS

We are not far from a market in transportation even under the current rules of open access transportation. A few simple steps, like vesting tradeable transportation rights in the holders of transportation contracts and granting the flexibility to subdivide, combine and transfer capacity, can take us to a market for natural gas transportation. A market in transportation decentralizes rate making and the allocation of transportation and enlists the power of networks to prevent monopolization.

Policy should aim at real tests of natural monopoly. Parallel regulated and unregulated systems would make the test real. Allow real tests of options by permitting contestable markets and contracts. Let pipelines make money and take risk. Take the risk off the core unless they willingly contract to assume it. Let joint ventures spread.

Regulated and unregulated segments of the transportation industry would operate in parallel. The supply of transportation capacity to the regulated sector will depend on the terms of the regulatory contract. The demand for the services which the regulatory agency contracts to supply will depend on the value of those services relative to what the unregulated sector supplies. Because it will not be possible to enlist users in contracts that cross-subsidize other users, subsidies will have to come directly from the agency's budget. This budget constraint will force some hard thinking about what the agency's product is and will make subsidies explicit.

Policy should promote the evolution of firms and industry organization; it should integrate the pipeline network by making network access a tradeable asset. Then firms and the industry can restructure themselves to use network resources. An effective and adaptive natural gas industry demands new and flexible institutions. It is unlikely that these institutions can be designed by regulators or other "outside" policy makers.

The industry is too complex for the centralized planning of structure that has characterized regulation in gas. Fixed structures are not adaptive. Policy that aims at a social optimum is too vague. Policy that aims at a specific goal is too narrow. A policy that aims at a static efficiency lacks robustness; it will be far from efficient when circumstances change.

It is not a mechanical world. Regulation is not just fine tuning of the mechanistic and predictable behavior of a monopolist. Markets do not just solve simultaneous equations more easily than a central planner; they discover information and provide the incentives to use it. Order comes from learning and feedback, and markets do this far better than any regulator could ever hope to do. The failing of regulation is that it does not exploit evolution, and the catastrophic changes that we have seen in natural gas are testimony to the brittleness of the regulatory equilibrium. Our conclusion? Remove natural gas from the political agenda and turn it over to market forces.

NOTES

1. The endogenous emergence of institutions and patterns of interaction is known as *spontaneous order*. See Sugden (1989) and Hayek (1960, 1979).

2. This system is analyzed in more detail in De Vany (1993).

3. Bradley (1991) reports that there are fourteen hundred local distribution companies. At the first allocation, the capacity would pass from some twenty or so major pipelines to the local distribution companies. Subsequent reallocations would distribute capacity still more broadly.

4. This is proposed in two papers by Smith, De Vany, and Michaels (1988, 1990) and is part of Transcontinental Gas Pipe Line Corporation's restructuring proposal (1988).

5. See Rassenti, Smith, and McCabe (1994).

6. Ellig and High (1992) discuss some of the problems and prospects of a regulatory contract.

7. See Bradley (1993).

8. Ellig (undated) cites the California Public Utilities Commission's frank admission that it fought new pipelines so that residential customers would not end up paying for capacity that could be used to serve other markets.

9. Citizens Resources, a nonprofit corporation in Massachusetts, has taken advantage of its state's transport programs to deliver well-head purchases to low-income users.

Appendix: Accessibility Matrices

The accessibility matrices for 1986 and 1988 are given in the Tables A.1 and A.2.[1] Table 3.1 shows what basins and pipelines are in the sample and when they opened (both application and approval dates of open access status are shown). Corresponding to these changes in the network are the number of points to which each point can ship gas (out degrees) and the number of sources that can ship gas into that point (in degrees).

---

[1]The rows and columns of the accessibility matrices are not labeled, but they correspond to the pipelines listed in Table 3.1.

Table A.1
Pipeline Network Accessibility Matrix, 1986

1	0	0	0	0	0	0	0	0	0	0	0	0	0	0	0	0	0	0	0
0	1	0	0	0	0	0	0	0	0	0	0	0	0	0	0	0	0	0	0
0	0	1	1	1	1	1	1	1	1	1	0	0	1	0	0	0	1	1	1
0	0	1	1	1	1	0	0	0	1	1	1	1	1	1	1	1	0	0	0
0	0	1	1	1	1	0	0	0	1	1	1	1	1	1	1	1	0	0	0
0	0	1	1	1	1	0	0	0	1	1	0	0	0	1	0	0	0	0	0
0	0	0	0	0	0	1	0	0	0	0	0	0	0	0	0	0	0	0	0
0	0	1	1	1	1	1	1	1	1	1	0	0	0	0	0	0	1	1	1
0	0	0	0	0	0	0	1	1	0	1	0	0	0	0	0	0	1	1	1
0	0	1	1	1	1	1	1	1	1	0	1	0	0	0	0	0	1	1	1
0	0	1	1	1	1	0	0	0	1	1	1	1	1	1	1	1	0	0	0
0	0	0	0	0	0	0	0	0	0	0	1	0	0	0	0	0	0	0	0
0	0	0	1	0	0	0	0	0	0	1	1	1	1	1	1	1	0	0	0
0	0	1	1	1	1	0	0	0	1	1	1	1	1	1	1	1	0	0	0
0	0	0	0	0	0	0	0	0	0	0	0	0	1	0	0	0	0	0	0
0	0	1	1	1	1	0	0	0	1	1	1	1	1	1	1	1	0	0	0
0	0	0	0	0	0	0	0	0	0	0	0	0	0	0	0	1	0	0	0
0	0	0	0	0	0	0	0	0	0	0	0	0	0	0	0	0	1	0	0
0	0	1	0	0	0	1	1	1	1	0	0	0	0	0	0	0	1	1	1
0	0	1	0	0	0	1	1	1	1	0	0	0	0	0	0	0	1	1	1

Table A.2
Pipeline Network Accessibility Matrix, 1988

```
1 1 0 0 0 0 0 0 0 0 0 0 0 0 0 0 0 0 0 0
1 1 0 0 0 0 0 0 0 0 0 0 0 0 0 0 0 0 0 0
0 0 1 1 1 1 1 1 1 1 1 0 0 1 0 0 0 1 1 1
0 0 1 1 1 1 0 0 0 1 1 1 1 1 1 1 1 0 0 0
0 0 1 1 1 1 0 0 0 1 1 1 1 1 1 1 1 0 0 0
0 0 1 1 1 1 0 0 0 1 1 0 0 0 1 0 0 0 0 0
0 0 1 1 1 1 1 1 1 1 0 0 0 0 0 0 0 1 1 1
0 0 1 1 1 1 1 1 1 1 1 0 0 0 0 0 0 1 1 1
0 0 0 0 0 0 0 1 1 0 1 0 0 0 0 0 0 1 1 1
0 0 1 1 1 1 1 1 1 1 0 1 0 0 0 0 0 1 1 1
0 0 1 1 1 1 0 0 0 1 1 1 1 1 1 1 1 0 0 0
0 0 0 1 1 0 0 0 0 0 0 1 1 1 1 1 1 0 0 0
0 0 0 1 0 0 0 0 0 0 0 1 1 1 1 1 1 0 0 0
0 0 1 1 1 1 0 0 0 1 1 1 1 1 1 1 1 0 0 0
0 0 0 0 0 0 0 0 0 0 0 1 1 1 1 1 1 0 0 0
0 0 1 1 1 1 0 0 0 1 1 1 1 1 1 1 1 0 0 0
0 0 1 1 1 1 0 0 0 1 1 1 1 1 1 1 1 0 0 0
0 0 1 0 0 0 1 1 1 1 0 0 0 0 0 0 0 1 1 1
0 0 1 0 0 0 1 1 1 1 0 0 0 0 0 0 0 1 1 1
0 0 1 0 0 0 1 1 1 1 0 0 0 0 0 0 0 1 1 1
```

Bibliography

Akaike, H. (1973) Information theory and the extension of the maximum likelihood principle. In Petrov, B. and Csaki, F., editors, *2nd International Symposium on Information Theory*, 267–281, Budapest: Akademiai Kiado.

Alger, D. and Toman, M. (1990) Market-based regulation of natural gas pipelines. *Journal of Regulatory Economics* 2(3):262–280.

Baumol, W., Panzar, J., and Willig, R. (1988) *Contestable Markets and the Theory of Industry Structure.* Orlando, Fla.: Harcourt, Brace Jovanovich.

Belsley, D., Kuh, E., and Welsch, R. (1980) *Regression Diagnostics, Identifying Influential Data and Sources of Collinearity.* New York: Wiley.

Box, G. and Jenkins, G. (1970) *Time Series Analysis.* San Francisco: Holden Day.

Bradley, Jr., R. L. (1991) Reconsidering the natural gas act. Issue paper no. 5. Southern Regulatory Policy Institute.

Bradley, Jr., R. L. (1993) Deregulatory dynamics: Bypass and reckoning in the California natural gas market. Paper presented at the DOE/NARUC conference, New Orleans, Louisiana, April 27.

Cooley, T. F. and LeRoy, S. F. (1985) Atheoretical macroeconometrics: A critique. *Journal of Monetary Economics* 16:283–308.

Cramer, C. (1991) The economic effects of unbundled transportation services in the natural gas pipeline industry. *Transportation Journal* 31(2):24–32.

Daggett, S. (1955) *Principles of Inland Transportation*, 5th ed. Berkeley: University of California Press.

De Canio, S. J. (1990) Cross-contract crediting under FERC Order 500. *Contemporary Policy Issues* 8(2):159–175.

De Canio, S. J. and Frech, H. E. (1993) Vertical contracts: A natural experiment in gas pipeline regulation. *Journal of Institutional and Theoretical Economics* 149(2):370–372.

De Vany, A. S. (1993) A brave new world: Private contracting as a regulatory alternative. Paper presented at Cato Institute Conference on New Horizons in Natural Gas Deregulation, Washington D.C.

De Vany, A. S. and Walls, W. D. (1992) When barriers to markets fall: Pipeline deregulation, spot markets, and the topology of the natural gas market. Working paper no. 123. Transportation Center, University of California, Berkeley.

De Vany, A. S. and Walls, W. D. (1993) Pipeline access and market integration in the natural gas industry: Evidence from cointegration tests. *The Energy Journal* 14(4):1–19.

De Vany, A. S. and Walls, W. D. (1994a) Natural gas industry transformation, competitive institutions and the role of regulation: Lessons from open access in U.S. natural gas markets. *Energy Policy* 22(9):755–763.

De Vany, A. S. and Walls, W. D. (1994b) Network connectivity and price convergence: Gas pipeline deregulation. *Research in Transportation Economics* 3:1–36.

De Vany, A. S. and Walls, W. D. (1994c) Open access and the emergence of a competitive natural gas market. *Contemporary Economic Policy* 12(2):77–96.

Dearborn, N. W. (1990) The developing natural gas futures market and its potential impact on domestic natural gas markets. *Natural Gas Monthly*, 1–21.

Doane, M. J. and Spulber, D. F. (1992) Open access and the evolution of the U.S. spot market for gas. Paper presented at International Association for Energy Economics, 14th Annual North American Conference.

Ellig, J. (undated) Taxation and regulation by Tiebout duopoly: The case of the Southern California gas market. Mimeograph, The Independent Institute.

Ellig, J. and High, J. (1992) Social contracts and pipe dreams. *Contemporary Policy Issues* 10(1):39–51.

Engle, R. F. and Granger, C. (1987) Co-integration and error correction: Representation, estimation, and testing. *Econometrica* 55:251–276.

Engle, R. F. and Yoo, B. S. (1987) Forecasting and testing in co-integrated systems. *Journal of Econometrics* 35:143–159.

Federal Energy Regulatory Commission (1991) Notice of proposed rulemaking. Docket no. RM91-11-000, Issued July 31.

Federal Energy Regulatory Commission (1993) Report of Commissioner Branko Terzic Chairman FERC Pipeline Competition Task Force on Competition in Natural Gas Transportation. Office of Economic Policy, FERC, May 24.

Gallick, E. C. (1993) *Competition in the Natural Gas Pipeline Industry: An Economic Policy Analysis.* Westport, Conn.: Praeger.

Harvey, A. C. (1981) *Time Series Models.* Oxford: Philip Allan.

Hayek, F. (1960) *The Constitution of Liberty.* London: Routledge and Kegan.

Hayek, F. (1973–1979) *Law, Legislation and Liberty,* 3 vols. London: Routledge and Kegan.

Hubbard, R. G. and Weiner, R. J. (1986) Regulation and long-term contracting in the U.S. natural gas market. *Journal of Industrial Economics* 35:71–79.

Hubbard, R. G. and Weiner, R. J. (1991) Efficient contracting and market power: Evidence from the U.S. natural gas industry. *Journal of Law and Economics* 34:25–68.

Kahn, A. (1988) *The Economics of Regulation.* Cambridge, Mass.: MIT Press.

Kloek, T. and Van Dijk, H. (1978) Bayesian estimates of equation system parameters: An application of integration by Monte Carlo. *Econometrica* 46:1–20.

Lütkepohl, H. (1991) *Introduction to Multivariate Time Series Analysis.* Berlin: Springer-Verlag.

Lyon, T. P. and Hackett, S. C. (1993) Bottlenecks and governance structures: Open access and long-term contracts for natural gas. *Journal of Law and Economic Organization* 9(2): 380–398.

Lyon, T. P. and Toman, M. A. (1991) Designing price caps for gas distribution systems. *Journal of Regulatory Economics* 3:175–192.

MacAvoy, P. A. and Pindyck, R. S. (1975) *The Economics of the Natural Gas Shortage (1960-1980).* New York: North Holland.

MacKinnon, J. (1990) Critical values for cointegration tests. Working paper. University of California, San Diego.

Mahoney, J. (1985) *Intermodal Freight Transportation.* Westport, Conn.: Eno Foundation.

Masten, S. E. (1988) Minimum bill contracts: Theory and policy. *Journal of Industrial Economics* 37:85–97.

Masten, S. E. and Crocker, K. J. (1985) Efficient adaptation in long-term contracts: Take-or-pay for natural gas. *American Economic Review* 75(5): 1083–1093.

Mulherin, J. (1986a) Complexity in long term natural gas contracts: An analysis of natural gas contractual provisions. *Journal of Law and Economic Organization* 2:105–117.

Mulherin, J. (1986b) Specialized assets, governmental regulation, and organizational structure in the natural gas industry. *Journal of Institutional and Theoretical Economics* 142:528–541.

Osterwald-Lenum, M. (1992) A note with quantiles of the asymptotic distribution of the maximum likelihood cointegration rank test statistics. *Oxford Bulletin of Economics and Statistics* 54(3):461–471.

Rassenti, S. J., Smith, V. L. and McCabe, K. (1994) Designing a real time computer assisted auction for natural gas networks. In Cooper, W. and Whinston, A., editors, *New Directions in Computational Economics*, 41–54, London: Kluwer.

Scherer, F. M. (1980) *Industrial Market Structure and Economic Performance*, 2nd ed. Boston: Houghton Mifflin.

Schwarz, G. (1978) Estimating the dimension of a model. *Annals of Statistics* 6:461–464.

Smith, R. T. (1988) *Trading Water: An Economic and Legal Framework for Water Marketing.* Washington D.C.: Council of State and Policy Planning Agencies.

Smith, R. T., De Vany, A. S., and Michaels, R. J. (1988) An Open Access Rights System for natural gas pipelines. In *Interstate Natural Gas Pipeline Rate Design Studies.* Washington D.C.: Natural Gas Supply Association.

Smith, R. T., De Vany, A. S., and Michaels, R. J. (1990) Defining a right of access to interstate natural gas pipelines. *Contemporary Policy Issues* 8:142–158.

Sugden, R. (1989) Spontaneous order. *Journal of Economic Perspectives* 3(4):85–97.

Tussing, A. R. and Barlow, C. C. (1984) *The Natural Gas Industry: Evolution, Structure and Economics.* Cambridge: Ballinger.

U.S. Energy Information Administration (1989) *Growth in Unbundled Natural Gas Transportation Services: 1982-1987.* Washington, D.C.: U.S. GPO.

Walls, W. D. (1992) *Open Access Transportation, Network Competition, and Market Integration in the Natural Gas Pipeline Industry.* Ph.D. dissertation, University of California.

Walls, W. D. (1993) A note on the natural gas futures market. *Pacific and Asian Journal of Energy* 3(2):221–228.

Walls, W. D. (1994a) A cointegration rank test of market linkages with an application to the U.S. natural gas industry. *Review of Industrial Organization* 9:181–191.

Walls, W. D. (1994b) Competition and prices in the deregulated gas pipeline network: A multivariate cointegration analysis. *The Journal of Energy and Development*, forthcoming.

Walls, W. D. (1994c) Price convergence across natural gas production fields and city markets. *The Energy Journal* 15(4):37–48.

Walls, W. D. (1995) An econometric analysis of the market for natural gas futures. *The Energy Journal* 16(1).

Index

About the Authors

ARTHUR S. DE VANY is Professor of Economics and a member of the Institute for Mathematical Behavioral Science at the University of California, Irvine.

W. DAVID WALLS is Assistant Professor of Economics at the School of Economics and Finance at the University of Hong Kong.

ISBN 0-89930-944-5

EAN

9 780899 309446

90000>

HARDCOVER BAR CODE